W9-BRN-927

THE GONE FISHIN' PORTFOLIO

Get Wise, Get Wealthy—and Get On with Your Life

ALEXANDER GREEN

WILEY

John Wiley & Sons, Inc.

For general information on our other products and services or for technical support, please contact our Customer Care Department within the United States at (800) 762-2974, outside the United States at (317) 572-3993, or fax (317) 572-4002.

Wiley also publishes its books in a variety of electronic formats. Some content that appears in print may not be available in electronic books. For more information about Wiley products, visit our Web site at www.wiley.com.

Library of Congress Cataloging-in-Publication Data:
Green, Alexander, 1958-
   The gone fishin' portfolio : get wise, get wealthy-- and get on with your life / Alexander Green.
      p. cm.
   Includes index.
   ISBN 978-0-470-11267-0 (cloth)
  1. Investments. 2. Portfolio management. 3. Finance, Personal. I. Title.
   HG4521.G693 2008
   332.6—dc22   2008017690

10 9 8 7 6 5 4 3 2 1

This book is dedicated to Judith and Braxton Green. If there is one thing I know how to do, it's pick the right parents.

If a man writes a book, let him set down only what he knows. I have guesses enough of my own.

Johann Wolfgang von Goethe

CONTENTS

FOREWORD

You have no idea what good hands you're in. I do . . .

You see, at this point I'm now one of the world's most widely read investment analysts. I'm not quite sure how I got here. I don't have a gimmick. I don't promise zillion-percent returns overnight. I think I'm here because I've given consistently good advice over my career.

One of the best pieces of advice I can give you today is this: Listen to Alex Green.

I know that Alex Green is better than I am at what I do. Darn it, the guy always has been.

I started out in the business as an investment advisor. Alex worked at the same firm. It was obvious why people trusted him with their life's savings, and why, too, he was in a league of his own.

You see, Alex has an extraordinary ability to see an investment idea before anyone else. And he combines that with another extraordinary ability—he can communicate complicated investment ideas in plain language.

Sometimes I'd sit in his office and just listen to him talk to his clients. I'd go back to my desk inspired and try to emulate him. But I couldn't come close.

I concluded that Alex's brain somehow works a hair quicker than even the smartest of us.

I've accomplished everything you can in the investment world. I've got a Ph.D. in this stuff, I've worked for a billion-dollar New York hedge fund, and I've literally traveled the world sizing up investments—going to places as extreme as Iceland and Ecuador, and discovering big opportunities. Today, hundreds of thousands of people rely on my investment advice. And I'm confident I'm good at what I do.

I know I'm smart. I know I make consistently good decisions. But my experience is, Alex Green is one step ahead of me.

How does he do it? I don't know. And it all looks so easy too . . . because it is for him. He just loves to soak everything up. But the nice thing about Alex is, none of this goes to his head.

This book, *The Gone Fishin' Portfolio*, is classic Alex. Since it's his first book, the temptation had to be great for him to dazzle you with all he knows. Instead, he took the opposite approach.

He clearly asked himself, "What is the simplest, most useful piece of investment advice I can share with a wide audience of investors?"

The answer is what you have in your hands right now.

In my view, most of the books in the investment section of your local bookstore are garbage. They're either too simplistic or too pie-in-the-sky. More often than not, you finish them and ask yourself, "Now what do I do?"

This book is different—and rare. It provides a simple but sophisticated strategy that actually works, written in plain language, by a brilliant investor.

And you won't wonder what to do. He tells you what to do, very specifically. He shows you exactly where to put your money and in what percentages. He also tells you what you need to do to keep your portfolio on track. It takes only a few minutes a year. What's not to like?

When I say you are in good hands with Alex Green, I'm saying it from deep down in my toes. I don't offer up praise lightly. But I have known him for over 15 years, and I can confidently say that Alex is as smart an investor as you'll ever find.

If you want to make more money safely from your investments, you really can't do better than Alex Green. Believe me; I've tried.

DR. STEVE SJUGGERUD
Editor, *True Wealth*
April 24, 2008
St. Helier, New Jersey

PREFACE

In July 2001, I retired from the securities industry at the ripe old age of 43. After 16 years as an investment advisor, research analyst, and portfolio manager, I had gone from a net worth of approximately zero to financial independence.

I was now free to do whatever I wanted, wherever I wanted, with whomever I wanted. It's called total financial freedom. And I can tell you from experience, it's a great feeling.

Unfortunately, many of my clients had not become financially independent. This was not because I advised them poorly. As an investment advisor, I dealt with my clients honestly and gave them the best advice and service I could.

Yet, in many ways, they operated at a disadvantage. Some clients had a poor understanding of investment fundamentals. Others found it impossible to commit to a long-term investment plan. Many were simply too emotional about the markets, running to cash at the first hint of danger.

Contrarian instincts are rare, too, I learned. Few people are emotionally stirred by low stock prices. But I am one of them. Every time there was a correction, a crash, or financial panic, my

Scottish blood would surge, my pulse would rise, I'd rub my hands together, and start buying.

My clients often did just the opposite. They were more inclined to curse loudly, sleep little, and hurl epithets, some unrepeatable. Unfortunately, strong emotions like these are often a prelude to bad investment decisions.

Then there was the other small matter of my firm's fee schedule. Investment professionals don't get into the industry because the work is meaningful but low paying. You become a broker, a financial planner, an insurance agent, or a money manager to get rich. And most of us do, eventually. In truth, what you're paying your financial advisor is probably too much. Many investors aren't doing that well because their advisor is doing *too well*.

This story is as old as Wall Street itself. In his book *Where Are the Customers' Yachts?*, originally published in 1940, Fred Schwed Jr. tells the story of a visitor to New York who is taken to the harbor and shown the impressive yachts that belong to the bankers and brokers. A tad naive, the visitor asks, "but where are the customers' yachts?"

Where indeed.

I'm not suggesting this is all Wall Street's fault. Clients are rarely abducted and forced at gunpoint to sign account-opening forms. Nor can advisors make important investment decisions without their clients' consent (not without landing in the hoosegow, anyway). We all need to take responsibility for the decisions we've made, including the decision to delegate important responsibilities.

Since retiring from life as a registered investment advisor seven years ago, I've been busy living what I call "the second half of my life." I've been writing about the financial markets for Agora Publishing, the world's largest publisher of investment letters.

Currently, I am the investment director of The Oxford Club, the world's largest financial fellowship with over 70,000 members. I am also chairman of Investment U, an Internet-based investment research service with over 300,000 subscribers. (As a sideline, I also write *Spiritual Wealth,* a twice-weekly e-letter dedicated to ideas about how to live a richer, more meaningful life Feel free to check it out at SpiritualWealth.com. It's free.)

Frankly, being a writer instead of an investment advisor suits me better. I can give advice freely and no one who heeds it has to wonder whether my real motive is to earn fees or commissions or "capture their assets." I can write what I want about the market without a compliance officer scrutinizing my words. And my readers don't have to worry about the objectivity of my analysis. I have no business relationships with the companies I cover, no investment banking colleagues seeking customers for new bond issues or secondary offerings, no reason to tell anything but the plain truth as I see it.

I don't mind telling you that many of these truths I learned the hard way. You can save yourself a lot of trouble—not to mention a boatload of money—by learning from my experience. As I've told my regular readers, "I've made the dumb mistakes so you don't have to."

In the pages that follow, I'm going to share with you the best long-term investment strategy I know. I call it the Gone Fishin' Portfolio.

This portfolio will allow you to successfully manage your money yourself using a simple yet highly sophisticated strategy to increase your returns, reduce your investment risk, eliminate Wall Street's high fees, and keep the taxman at bay, too. The idea is simple: to "Get Wise, Get Wealthy—and Get On with Your Life."

In Part I, **Get Wise**, we'll examine the challenges you face as an investor. I'll review the fundamental relationship between risk and reward in the financial markets. You'll also get an insider's view of how the investment industry *really* works.

Get Wealthy, discussed in Part II, means understanding and, I hope, adopting the Gone Fishin' strategy. You'll learn why this is arguably the safest and simplest way to reach your long-term financial goals. I will also address the financial and psychological challenges you're likely to face in the years ahead.

Get On with Your Life, which we will discuss in Part III, means taking your financial destiny into your hands and, at the same time, reclaiming your most precious resource—your time.

Setting up the Gone Fishin' Portfolio is a snap. Maintaining it takes less than 20 minutes a year.

You may not believe you're qualified to manage your money yourself. If so, I beg to differ. Investing can be made endlessly complicated, or breathtakingly simple. If you're willing to keep things simple, you're perfectly qualified to manage your money yourself—and in a highly sophisticated way.

As an investor, your overriding goal is to achieve and maintain financial independence. Your savings are the fuel. The Gone Fishin' Portfolio is the vehicle to get you there.

Let's get started.

ACKNOWLEDGMENTS

Many of the lessons in this book came with a knock to the head. Still, I did learn. So I'm grateful for those who gave me that opportunity.

Diego Veitia hired me to become a registered representative back before I knew a stock from a bond. (Pity my early clients.) Without this initial opportunity, I may never have had a career in the financial markets. Thank you, Diego, for taking a chance on me.

I'd also like to thank Mark Skousen, a first-rate economist, author, lecturer, libertarian, and friend. He has taught me a lot about free minds and free markets.

It has also been my exceptional good fortune to work with Bill Bonner, Mark Ford, Julia Guth, and my other colleagues, mentors, and good friends at Agora Publishing. Agora is not only the world's largest publisher of investment letters, it is also one of the world's most entrepreneurial companies. What an amazing group of bright, creative, hard-working, (and loony), people.

Writing a book is a bigger project than I would have imagined when I undertook this one. I'd like to thank Mike Ward for nudging me (nagging, really) to take this road. I'd also like to thank

Matt Weinschenk and Bob Williams for their many hours of help, research, and support in the shaping and editing of this book.

Thanks, too, to my publishers and editors at John Wiley & Sons, including Debra Englander and Kelly O'Connor, who reviewed the manuscript and recommended many important changes and clarifications.

I want to express my love and appreciation to my wife Karen, daughter Hannah, and son David, who often asked, "Where's Dad?" during the writing process. Without their patience and support, this book would never have been written.

Lastly, I would like to thank all my regular readers at The Oxford Club, Investment U, and *Spiritual Wealth,* as well as anyone taking the time to read this book.

Carpe Diem.

ALEX GREEN

PART I

Get Wise

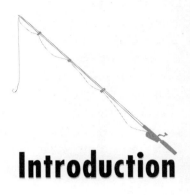

Introduction

As an investment analyst, I speak frequently at investment conferences across the United States and around the world.

The attendees come for a number of different reasons. Some want to gain some insights on interest rates, the dollar, or the stock market. Others are seeking a new investment strategy. Still others are looking for good investment ideas or, as one gentleman insisted, "just one great stock."

But before you can put your money to work effectively, you need something even more fundamental to your success: a philosophy of investing.

In her book *Philosophy: Who Needs It*, Ayn Rand argues that all of us have a philosophy of life, whether we know it or not. "Your only choice," she writes, "is whether you define your philosophy by a conscious, rational, disciplined process of thought . . . or let your subconscious accumulate a junk heap of unwarranted conclusions . . . "

What's true of life is also true of investing.

Over the past two decades, I've dealt with thousands of individual investors, some highly astute, some rank novices. Many had only the foggiest notion of what they were trying to achieve—or how. In some ways this is understandable. World financial markets are complex and the investment process can be daunting.

Beginners often don't understand the fundamentals of saving and investing. And even more experienced investors are often stymied by the complexities and technical jargon surrounding the investment process. Many try (and inevitably fail) to outguess the markets—or simply wave the white flag and turn their portfolio over to "that nice young man down at Merrill Lynch."

Big mistake.

No one cares more about your money than you do. With a basic understanding of the investment process and a bit of discipline, you're perfectly capable of managing your own money, even your "serious money." *Especially* your serious money. By managing your own money, you'll be able to earn higher returns and save many thousands of dollars in investment costs over your lifetime.

The Gone Fishin' Portfolio rests on a powerful philosophy of investing. It's battle-tested. It's built on the most advanced—and realistic—theories of money management. And it works.

Moreover, this book does something that virtually no other investment guide does. I'm going to show you—very specifically—where you should put your money. And then I'm going to show you how to manage it year after year.

Once you've set up your portfolio, the whole process will take less than 20 minutes a year to implement. This may sound like an audacious claim. But, as you'll soon see, the strategy itself is steeped in humility.

It is based on the only realistic premise for an investment philosophy—that, to a great extent, the future is unknowable. So don't expect me to draw on my gift of prophecy and tell you what's going to happen to the economy, interest rates, the dollar, or world stock markets. (No one is more surprised than me how the market action unfolds each year.) Nor will we ignore uncertainty or pretend we have a system that has eliminated it. Instead, we're going to use uncertainty and make it our friend. In short, we're going to capitalize on it.

Investing is serious business. Getting it right is the difference between a retirement spent in comfort (or luxury) and spending your golden years counting nickels, worrying whether you'll have enough. The difference could hardly be starker.

Up until now, you may have been tempted to turn your investment portfolio over to someone else to manage. After all, your financial security is paramount. You may not think you can take the risk—or handle the responsibility—of running your money yourself. I fully intend to disabuse you of that notion. I also want to point out that there are serious risks to turning your money over to someone else. That person may manage it poorly. Or be terribly expensive. Or both.

If you're skeptical on this point, it may be that you've bought the story that Wall Street is selling: Investing is so complicated—or your personal circumstances so exceptional—that you should not be trusted to run your own money.

I'll concede that if you don't know what the heck you're doing, this is absolutely true. But one solution is learning what to do, rather than turning your financial welfare over to someone else.

When it comes to managing your money, there are plenty of potential pitfalls out there. However, those investors who wind up in retirement with less money than they need have generally fallen prey to one of four basic mistakes:

1. *They were too conservative,* so their portfolio didn't grow enough to begin generating the income required to meet their spending requirements.
2. *They were too aggressive,* so a significant percentage of their portfolio went up in flames along the way.
3. *They tried—and failed—to time the market.* Confident that they would be in for market rallies and out for market corrections, they ended up doing just the opposite much of the time.
4. *They delegated unwisely.* They turned their financial affairs over to a broker, insurance agent, or financial planner who—over time—converted a substantial amount of their assets into his assets. In addition, the advisor may have been too conservative, too aggressive, or tried and failed to time the market.

If your nest egg is lying in pieces late in life, you generally don't have the opportunity—or the time—to build another one. The consequences, both personal and financial, can be devastating.

Planning your financial future is a momentous responsibility. Although *The Gone Fishin' Portfolio* has a light-hearted name, it enables you to handle your serious money—the money you need to live on in retirement—in a serious way.

There are few guarantees in the world of investing. In fact, once you get beyond the risk-free world of Treasuries and certificates of deposit, there are virtually none. However, the Gone Fishin' Portfolio eliminates six major investment risks:

1. It keeps you from being so conservative that your long-term purchasing power fails to keep up with inflation.
2. It prevents you from handling your money recklessly.
3. It does not require you to own any individual stocks or bonds. So a single security—think Worldcom or Enron—cannot cause your portfolio to crater.
4. It does not require a broker, financial consultant, or anyone else to attach himself to your portfolio like a barnacle, siphoning off fees every year.
5. It doesn't require you—or any investment "expert"—to forecast the economy, predict the market, or analyze competing economic theories about the future.
6. Perhaps most importantly, it guarantees that your time will be your own. Rather than spending countless hours evaluating stocks, market trends, or fund managers, you'll spend your time as you please. While others struggle to manage their money effectively, you'll have "gone fishin'."

This last point means that instead of spending countless hours fretting over your investment portfolio, you'll be able to relax, . . . play golf . . . travel the world . . . spend more time with your kids or grandkids . . . or just swing on a hammock in the shade with a glass of ice-cold lemonade. Because your investments will be on autopilot.

This is not just a strategy for today's markets, incidentally. The Gone Fishin' Portfolio is designed to prosper—and generate peace of mind—through all market environments. And I invite you to be skeptical. In fact, let me begin by asking you a question:

If I could show you a way to manage your money yourself, using a strategy that is as powerful and effective as any used by the nation's top institutions, that will allow you to outperform the vast majority of investment professionals, pay nothing in sales charges, brokerage fees, or commissions, that will take less than 20 minutes a year to implement, and is based on an investment strategy so sophisticated it won the Nobel Prize in economics, would you be interested?

I hope so. That, in a nutshell, is the Gone Fishin' Portfolio. It's about handling the money you intend to retire on simply, effectively, and cost-efficiently, with the absolute minimum of time and attention.

If you're like most people I know, you have better things to do than watch your stocks bounce up and down all day.

Don't get me wrong. I'm not averse to trading stocks, myself. (Long-term investing and short-term trading are not mutually exclusive.) But short-term trading strategies are beyond the scope of this book. Instead of focusing on trading or speculating, we're going to focus here on the money you intend to retire on—and perhaps ultimately leave to your kids, your grandkids, or your favorite charity. This is money that shouldn't be treated like chips in a poker game.

Reaching financial independence is a serious goal, one that should be pursued in a disciplined, rigorous way.

That's why I recommend that you make the Gone Fishin' Portfolio the core of your long-term investment program. The philosophy behind it is based on the best investment thinking available. It has been tested in various economic conditions. It increases your returns while reducing your risk. And it minimizes your investment costs and annual capital gains taxes.

Best of all, it works. Investors who have put their money to work this way have enjoyed years of market-beating returns while taking less risk than being fully invested in stocks.

Now it's your turn.

CHAPTER 1

The Unvarnished Truth About Your Money

"I offer nothing more than simple facts, plain arguments, and common sense."

—Thomas Paine

Several years ago, some friends and I were vacationing in Key West and decided to do some deep-sea fishing.

We didn't have a boat, so we went to a local marina to see what we could charter. There were several boats available, so we began talking to various captains.

Most assured us that the fishing was excellent and encouraged us to hire them for the next day, before someone else booked them first. But since we were in no hurry, we took our time and kept wandering down the dock chatting with the crew of different charters.

Near the end of the dock, we saw an older captain leaning back comfortably in his captain's chair with a beer in one hand and a cigar in the other.

"How's the fishin' been lately?" I asked.

"The fishin's been great," he said. "But the catchin'," he added with a shake of his head, "the catchin' ain't been so good."

"Why not?" we asked, a little surprised given the positive spin we had gotten from the other boat captains.

He said the weather had been unseasonably cool. That had affected migration patterns. The big schools of fish hadn't shown up yet. "Nobody's been catchin' much lately," he said.

We looked at each other in disappointment.

"It's still great weather to go out," he added. "And the fish *might* show up," he said after a long puff on his cigar. "You never know."

The prospect of spending the afternoon on the water without catching anything more than a bout of sea sickness wasn't terribly appealing. So we huddled to talk about what we wanted to do. After a little discussion, we decided we were willing to risk going out. We also agreed we wanted to use the old boat captain.

Unlike the others, he hadn't blown any smoke up our skirts. He wasn't interested in talking us into a fishing trip. He didn't seem to particularly care whether we hired him or not. As a result, he did something nobody else did. He told us the truth. So we hired him.

We knew from the outset that we were running the risk of hiring a boat and sitting on the water all day without so much as a nibble. We could live with that. And, if we didn't catch anything, well, at least we went out with our eyes wide open.

The next day the weather was perfect. Despite his laid back attitude, the captain and his mate were good company and gave first-rate service. And the "catchin'?" It was the best fishing I'd ever experienced—then or since.

A few hours after he got us out to his "spot," the ocean suddenly filled with so many dolphin—mahi—that the water turned yellow.

After a couple hours, our arms were tired. We literally couldn't hoist any more in. When we returned to port, we were giving away fish to the crew, other anglers who had come back empty-handed, even strangers on the dock. Our coolers weren't big enough to hold them all. (And, in case you don't know, fresh Florida mahi is just about the best-tasting fish around.)

What does this story have to do with your investment portfolio? Not much, really. Except I'd like to do for you what that boat captain did for us that day. I want to tell you the unvarnished truth.

I'd like to help you meet your long-term investment goals. But I don't want to sell you a financial plan, charge you a commission or wrap fee, or manage your money. I don't want you to subscribe to a financial magazine or investment letter. I just want to give you the straight dope with no strings attached. Believe it or not, that's a rare thing in the world of investing.

LAY CLAIM TO WHAT'S YOURS

Think about it. When was the last time you received investment advice from someone who was both qualified to give it and had nothing to sell? Not a mutual fund, a trading service, a financial plan, a software program, a brokerage account, an insurance policy, a newsletter subscription, or a managed account. Nothing.

You might think you at least get independent investment advice from the national media, but think again. Cable television parades endless pundits across the screen, all with ever-changing opinions about the economy and the markets, all to sell advertising—most of it investment-related. The financial press maintains a circus of activity as well. Headlines shout, "Retire Rich," "Five Health Care Stocks to Buy Today," "Is This Bull Market Over?" "Double Your Investment Income," "The Shortcut to Seven Figures," and so on.

The Gone Fishin' Portfolio is an antidote to all this noise and confusion. It is the distillation of much of what I've learned over more than two decades as a research analyst, investment advisor, portfolio manager, and financial writer. It is the key to financial freedom—if you have the discipline to see it through. To benefit from this investment system, you need only follow three simple steps:

1. Read this book carefully to get a thorough understanding of how this strategy works—and why.
2. Put your money to work, as I suggest in Chapter 8.
3. Take less than 20 minutes a year to keep this system on track, as I describe in the same chapter.

That's it. If you follow these three simple steps, you'll be on your way to meeting your long-term financial goals—and spending about as much time on your portfolio each year as you would eating lunch at "Five Guys Famous Burgers and Fries."

Be forewarned that my objective here is not theoretical. I don't want you to simply read the book, nod your head, and say, "Good idea." My goal is to encourage you to use it, to benefit from it. I want to set you on a path to a place where money and its management are no longer a problem in your life.

In essence, the Gone Fishin' Portfolio is about setting you free from concerns about your financial future. True, the future is always uncertain. But you'll enjoy the satisfaction and peace of mind that come from using an investment system that offers a very high probability of success. That's not just my opinion, by the way. It's also the opinion of the Nobel Prize Committee. (More on that in Chapter 7.) Hundreds of billions of dollars of institutional money are being run using systems very similar to the one I'm about to describe.

Incidentally, I've also set up a special Web site devoted to this investment system. It will allow you to track your progress and even reminds you of the simple steps you need to take once a year to keep your portfolio on track. (Feel free to visit it at www.GoneFishinPortfolio.com.)

When you're done reading this book, there is only one commitment you'll need to make: personal responsibility for your own financial freedom. I can't overemphasize how important this is.

LEAVE NOTHING TO CHANCE

Your employer and the federal government are not going to get the job done for you. Yet for more than two-thirds of elderly Americans, Social Security is their major source of income. (For a third of them, Social Security is their only income.) If you are retired or close to it, you can count on Social Security to help meet your financial needs. But it's tough to imagine living on it.

For young workers, the program is a demographic time bomb. Americans are living healthier and longer lives than ever before.

When the Social Security program was created in 1935, a 65-year-old American had an average life expectancy of 12.5 years. Today, it is 18 years . . . and rising rapidly.

In addition, according to the U.S. Bureau of the Census, 78 million baby boomers began retiring in 2008. In 30 years, there will be twice as many Americans eligible for Social Security as there are today. Meanwhile, the number of workers per beneficiary has dropped from 5.1 in 1960, to 3.3 in 2007, to a projected 2.1 in 2032.

Forget about this so-called trust fund. Current payroll taxes are being used to pay out current benefits, making Social Security look increasingly like a Ponzi scheme. Early investors get paid by new ones. Latecomers get left holding the bag.

I'm not an alarmist, but facts are facts. There are not going to be enough workers to maintain the current level of benefits indefinitely. The federal government's own Web site says, "The current Social Security system is unsustainable in the long run."

Sure, the nation's number-one entitlement program will survive in some form. But the solution to the problem is likely to come in the form of higher payroll taxes, an increase in the age for eligibility, and fewer benefits. Of course, even in the most optimistic scenario, most of us can only count on Social Security to cover a small portion of our retirement expenses.

Private pension plans are going the way of the passenger pigeon, too. According to the Employee Benefit Research Institute, the share of private-sector workers covered by a pension has fallen from 39% in 1980 to 18% today. Nationwide, pensions are underfunded by more than $450 billion. Many corporations have raided their plans. Others have tried to chisel their way out of them. Some have simply waved the white flag and filed for bankruptcy.

Meanwhile, inflation—the thief that robs us all—is slowly but steadily driving up your cost of living. Your eroding purchasing power means you'll have to devote more of your budget in retirement to housing, utilities, insurance, health care costs, and other monthly expenses.

This may sound depressing. But by facing the music, you can start making the choices that will provide a comfortable retirement.

Unfortunately, polls show that over half of Americans believe it is the responsibility of the government or their employer to take care of them in retirement. These folks are in for one rude awakening.

You may indeed get benefits from your employer or the federal government. But neither will provide you with a cushy retirement.

That's up to you. As the American writer Elbert Hubbard said, "Responsibility is the price of freedom."

When you take control and accept full responsibility for your own financial welfare, you let go of the idea that it is someone else's obligation to provide for you in retirement. You let go of the idea that your broker or financial planner will ensure your financial independence.

Ultimately, your financial welfare is up to you. You need to plan. You need to save. And you need to manage your money intelligently. Fortunately, these are just the topics I'm going to cover in the pages ahead.

REEL IT IN...

1. The Gone Fishin' Portfolio is a powerful and effective, yet simple, investment system that can lead you to financial freedom.

2. You can enjoy a high probability of success using this investment approach, one that has garnered recognition from the Nobel Prize Committee and is being used—in similar fashion—by many of the world's biggest institutional investors.

3. The investing deck is fundamentally stacked against you. Brokers work for commissions. Planners want fees. And the national media seek advertisers and subscribers. Accordingly, the Gone Fishin' Portfolio is designed for investors seeking objectivity—the unvarnished truth—about their investments.

4. Don't depend on Uncle Sam for your retirement income. The federal government's own Web site says, "The current system is unsustainable in the long run."

5. Americans are living longer than ever. To live well in retirement, your portfolio needs to last as long as possible, too. And that's exactly the objective of the Gone Fishin' Portfolio.

CHAPTER 2

The First Step on the Road to Financial Freedom

"My problem lies with reconciling my gross habits with my net income."

—Errol Flynn

Before we explore the Gone Fishin' strategy, let's acknowledge a fundamental truth. There can be no investment without saving. I'm not talking about saving in terms of setting aside money for short-term goals like a new car or a down payment on a house. By saving, I mean giving up immediate spending in exchange for future income.

Saving for your future means setting aside enough money each month to reach your financial goals. Yes, it's partly about planning. But it's mostly about having the discipline to follow through.

However, a recent survey by mutual fund giant Fidelity Investments found that less than half (46%) of Americans are using an Individual Retirement Account. (Only 160 of 1,000 surveyed said they are very likely to contribute to an IRA.) Seven out of 10 eligible employees are using 401(k)s. Millions of workers are not preparing for retirement—or are giving up tax benefits.

Worse, a recent survey by Bankrate.com found that 68% of adults avoid news about the cost of retirement. Why do so many Americans have their heads in the sand? There are various reasons. Some see their parents living fairly well on Social Security and pensions. Others simply lack the discipline to save. In the Fidelity survey, only about a quarter said they would make a lifestyle change now to save for later.

These folks might want to go back and read Aesop's tale about the ant and the grasshopper. Thanks to healthier lifestyles and modern medicine, Americans are living longer than ever. In fact, according to Allstate, which has a vested interest in this sort of thing, the average 65-year-old woman can expect to live to 87, and the average 65-year-old man to 85.

If you're likely to live longer, you need a hard-working investment portfolio (one that can duck into a phone booth and come out with its cape unfurled). But to truly maximize the size of that portfolio, you're going to need to save as much as you can, as soon as you can, for as long as you can.

Most people know this, of course. They just have trouble doing it.

However, more Americans are saving and investing than the press might lead you to believe. Never at a loss for a sensational story, the national media creates the impression that Americans are spending everything, swimming in debt, and saving nothing. "Savings at 74-Year Low" screams one Associated Press headline. Another says, "Official U.S. Savings Rate: Zero."

Are these headlines wrong? Technically, no. But these stories have been twisted into something more ominous than they really are.

These figures deal only with personal savings made after taxes. Most working Americans, however, sock away a portion of their paycheck each month in a 401(k). It comes out of their checks pretax, not after tax. So the federal government doesn't count that as savings.

If you and your spouse both work, you could be putting as much as $31,000 between you in a qualified retirement plan each year (plus another $10,000 if you're both over 50). Your employer may be providing thousands of dollars in matching funds, too. Yet, according to official government statistics, you've "saved" nothing.

When you get your paycheck, you probably make a mortgage payment. Part of that money goes to pay down the principal, which builds equity. (You may even pay off a little extra from time to time.) But money you put into a mortgage is treated by Uncle Sam as consumption. So, once again, none of this is "savings" according to official statistics.

If you're contributing to an IRA or 401(k), you're on the right path. If you can save 10% or more of your after-tax income too, that's even better.

Of course, some Americans aren't funding a 401(k) or doing any other saving. Some don't own homes and, of those who do, many aren't paying down their mortgages. Rather, they've been borrowing against their homes, adding debt.

However, these folks don't represent the national trend. According to the Federal Reserve, at the end of 2007, U.S. households' total net worth—the total value of all assets, including stocks, bonds, bank accounts, houses and retirement funds, after subtracting debt—was $57.72 trillion. That's $17.7 trillion higher than it was four years ago. And it's over seven times what total net worth was in the United States in 1980. Total American wealth is clearly rising, not falling.

But if you want to join that group whose net worth is rising the fastest, you probably need to save more.

SOMETIMES LESS IS MORE

In *The Millionaire Next Door*, Thomas Stanley reported that most Americans with a net worth of a million dollars or more follow a remarkably similar path. They maximize their earned income, minimize their expenses, live beneath their means, and religiously save the difference. It may sound pedestrian. But do this long enough and one day you just may wake up with a seven-figure net worth.

It means making sacrifices, however. As we go through life, we quickly learn that expenses seem to rise to meet the income available.

In our wonderful capitalistic society, there is never a shortage of fabulous products and services vying for our attention.

However, it *is* possible to say no.

A couple of years ago, I was invited to do a segment about saving and investing on Fox TV in Tampa. Near the end, the interviewer suddenly popped this question, "What do you say to those viewers out there who say they just can't save *anything?*"

As it happened, I had just returned from a two-week investment expedition to China. During my trip, I had visited with many laborers who made less than $150 a month. Yet the average Chinese worker—acutely aware that the government provides no social safety net—saves over 30% of his income. (I'm not suggesting an American could live on anything close to this. But it was a powerful lesson in fiscal discipline nonetheless.)

"Too many Americans don't save anything," I reminded the moderator, half-jokingly, "because they're spending money they don't have, on things they don't need, to impress people they don't like." Judging by the look on his face, that wasn't the answer he was expecting.

Look, I realize that when you're young and starting out in life, saving may not be a priority. When you get older and you have kids (and perhaps elderly parents) to support, saving can be tough, too.

But most of us could get by—by hook or by crook—on at least 10% less than what we're living on today. If we pay ourselves that 10% (or more) first, it will make a world of difference 10, 20, or 30 years down the road.

Of course, it's not hard times that keep most Americans from saving what they should. It's lack of discipline, something at which I used to excel.

As a young man in my twenties, I worked as a stockbroker in a local firm. I soon began earning a six-figure income. Not long after, I bought a brand-spanking-new lakefront house, got the ski boat, the Jaguar XJ-6, and all the other toys. I saved virtually nothing.

When my friends came over for parties—which were frequent—most of them assumed I was rich. I was nothing of the sort. Wealth is not the same thing as income. If you earn a lot of money and blow it every year, you're not rich. You're just living high. Wealth is what you accumulate, not what you earn. And it certainly can't be measured by what you spend.

TABLE 2.1 Effects of Saving $500 a Month for 30 Years at 10%

Year	Savings
1	$6,600.00
5	$40,294.00
10	$105,187.00
20	$378,015.00
30	$1,085,661.00

Fortunately, because I was working in the financial services industry, I learned the importance of saving before it was too late. Take a look at Table 2.1, for example. It demonstrates the enormous advantage of beginning to save early. No matter what your age, it's never too late to begin.

As Thomas T. Stanley and William D. Danko wrote in *The Millionaire Next Door*:

> Affluent people typically follow a lifestyle conducive to accumulating money. In the course of our investigations, we discovered seven common denominators among those who build wealth successfully.
>
> **1.** They live well below their means.
> **2.** They allocate their time, energy, and money efficiently, in ways conducive to building wealth.
> **3.** They believe that financial independence is more important than displaying high social status.
> **4.** Their parents did not provide economic outpatient care.
> **5.** Their adult children are economically self-sufficient.
> **6.** They are proficient in targeting market opportunities.
> **7.** They chose the right occupation.

In short, they discovered that your net worth is essentially a result of the choices you make. To save as much as you can, you need to make the right career decisions, the right lifestyle decisions, and the right spending decisions. It takes forethought. It takes discipline. And it means making hard choices.

If this sounds old-fashioned, so be it. Most of us are not talented enough to start the next computer company in our garage or play third base for the Yankees. Your income alone is not probably going to make you rich. So the quickest way to jumpstart your investment program is to start saving more.

A MATTER OF HOW WE VALUE THINGS

I realize you have to have balance in your life. You can't be happy—now or in retirement—living like a miser. The trick is to find the right balance between saving and spending. Each day there are choices you can make that will help you—or hinder you—on your way to financial independence.

If you keep in mind the choice between consumption and freedom, it becomes easier. Do you really need that new car—or would you rather keep the old one and become free to live where you want, with whom you want, doing what you want? Do you really need that new set of golf clubs—or would you rather keep your old ones and live where you want, with whom you want, doing what you want?

Ultimately, the choices are this stark. Because it doesn't matter how high the returns are on your investments are if you haven't saved enough. Or, worse, if you're trying to dig yourself out from under a mountain of debt.

If you're looking for a bit of inspiration, consider Billy and Akaisha Kaderli. Not long ago, they were profiled on both Kiplinger.com and Bankrate.com. The Kaderlis live in an adult-active community in Mesa, Arizona, even though they don't meet the community's minimum age requirements. Although they're now in their seventeenth year of retirement, the couple ditched the rat race when they were 38 years old.

When they first retired, the Kaderlis sold their home and simply explored the world, traveling between the Caribbean island of Nevis, Venezuela, Mexico, and Thailand.

Most folks would say they are living the dream, playing golf, traveling the world, and socializing with friends, whenever they want. How did they do it? Not by striking it rich, but by being frugal.

They are an example of what some call "extreme early retirement." In their late thirties, Billy and Akaisha decided they were working too much, enjoying it too little, and paying too much in taxes. Most of us would simply shrug and say, "That's life."

However, the Kaderlis decided financial freedom was a lot more important than accumulating more stuff. According to Akaisha, "Every time I looked at a latte or a new pair of shoes, I decided I didn't need them. If you're clear about what you want, it becomes easier. You can either buy this or be days closer to your goal."

Contrast this point of view with the materialistic mindset of many Americans, who often find themselves stuck on what psychologists call "the hedonic treadmill." Instead of thinking about financial freedom, they're obsessed with thoughts of a bigger house, a fancier car, the best new restaurants and, of course, a high-definition, 50-inch, flat-panel TV.

I won't argue that these things aren't desirable. And, who knows, a bigger house may be a great investment (although not lately, and particularly not if you pull the equity out and spend it). But if you want to enjoy extreme early retirement, the key is to earn as much as you can, spend as frugally as you can, and religiously save the difference.

The Kaderlis have set up a Web site (retireearlylifestyle.com) to share their wisdom and experience. They list five sensible steps to early retirement:

1. *Track spending.* Take a close look at your spending on a daily basis. Once you start doing so, you'll be amazed at what you're spending your money on. It only takes a few minutes a day once you set up your system. After a month or two, you'll discover where you can reduce your expenses. Within a year, you'll be in control of future spending.
2. *Save a lot.* Once you have control of your spending, save that extra money for your future. If you're younger than 30 years old, a good target is to save 10% of your gross income—not your take-home pay, but the full amount of your salary before taxes and other deductions. After a short time, you won't miss the difference, but your savings will grow substantially. If you're over 30, increase your savings rate to 15% or more if possible. Take full advantage of employer-sponsored plans like 401(k)s, matching

contributions, and any other retirement benefits you receive—but don't include them in your savings percentages. That should be on top of what you're already saving on your own.

3. *Invest wisely.* Learn about investments, become your own expert, and keep things simple. You don't need to impress your friends with financial terms just so you can look knowledgeable.

4. *Put peer pressure into perspective.* Social pressure to spend can be subtle and pervasive, and it can divert you from your commitment to retire early. Marketing specialists tell you that if you only buy this new product, car, house, or membership, your lifestyle will improve. It's reasonably easy to tune out that marketing message, but you have to handle your friends with a little more tact. Trying to match the spending of our peer group is a surefire way to derail financial goals. Decide now that you don't have to keep up with their consumption to fit into the crowd. The choice is yours—not theirs.

5. *Keep your eye on the prize.* Set realistic goals and keep to your plan. The amount you save, how you invest, and when you plan to retire may differ from your colleagues and others. No one will be as dedicated or determined as you are to reach your objectives. Put these goals somewhere where you'll see them often, to remind you to keep you on course. Every time you get sidetracked by spending a little bit more, succumbing to peer pressure, or choosing not to put extra money into your retirement funds, you're literally delaying your retirement date by weeks, months, or perhaps even years. Stay focused.

This is good, commonsense advice. And unlike the performance of the stock market, saving is something that is under your control. It's guaranteed to make a significant impact in the long-term value of your portfolio. And—trust me—it's a whole lot safer than attempting something heroic with your investments.

In short, a successful investment program begins with disciplined saving. Regular saving remains the safest, easiest, and most effective way to boost your portfolio. True, it means making hard choices. But, ultimately, you are the person responsible for your financial well-being.

Rare is the individual who stumbles on financial freedom accidentally. Unless you've got a rich relative with a bad heart—and a soft spot for you—whether you end up a slave to money or its master is likely to depend mostly on you, and the choices you make.

As Robert Louis Stevenson wrote 140 years ago, "Everybody, soon or late, sits down to a banquet of consequences."

REEL IT IN...

1. There can be no successful investment program without saving. And significant saving requires a measure of fiscal discipline.
2. A high percentage of American workers are not adequately saving, which impacts the likelihood of a sound retirement.
3. Participating in a 401(k) or IRA program is a great route to savings. But you should also save at least 10% of your after-tax income.
4. Most high-net-worth individuals did not strike it rich, but, rather, had the discipline to live beneath their incomes and save the difference between their net income and expenses.
5. Finding that perfect balance between saving and spending is key to living happily now and in retirement.
6. Saving generally means prioritizing financial freedom over high living.

CHAPTER 3

Why Manage Your Own Money?

"The great enemy of truth is very often not the lie—deliberate, contrived, and dishonest—but the myth—persistent, persuasive, and unrealistic."

—John F. Kennedy

"I was spreading some risk around, and apparently it all wound up in your portfolio."

Many investment books contain a chapter about how to find a qualified investment advisor. This one doesn't.

As I mentioned earlier, no one cares more about your money than you do. You should manage it yourself. By the time you finish this book, you'll be perfectly capable.

I'm not suggesting that investment advisors who are competent and ethical don't exist. They do. I've worked with some of them. In a former life, I was an investment advisor myself. I'd like to believe I was one of the good ones. It's just that most investors don't *need* to pay for the services of a good one, either.

This flies in the face of what Wall Street often tells you, that investing is so complicated that you *require* their services. Or that the higher returns investment professionals can deliver will more than cover the cost of their services. More often than not, this is an empty promise.

It's true that many people don't know enough to manage their own money. There is, however, a simple remedy for this. And this book aims to provide it. So don't let your full-service broker give you a low whistle and a shake of the head. Listen to those with a more independent frame of mind.

- Nobel Laureate Paul Samuelson has said, "It is not easy to get rich in Las Vegas, at Churchill Downs, or at the local Merrill Lynch office."
- Investment commentator Ben Stein writes, "Are you by chance a 'high-net-worth' individual? That special handling everyone is giving you is merely the anesthetic that precedes the surgical removal of your wallet."
- In *What Wall Street Doesn't Want You to Know*, Larry Swedroe says, "Wall Street does not have the best interests of investors at heart. Wall Street wants to keep individual investors in the dark about both the academic evidence on how markets really work and the dismal track record of the vast majority of active managers."
- Author Michael Lewis wrote in the December 2007 issue of *Condé Nast Portfolio*, "Wall Street, with its army of brokers, analysts, and advisers funneling trillions of dollars into mutual funds, hedge funds, and private equity funds, is an elaborate fraud."

- Author and investment advisor Phil DeMuth writes on his Web site (www.phildemuth.com/) "Sadly, the high-net-worth individual is often treated as little more than a cow hooked up to Wall Street's milking machine."
- Not to be outdone, William Bernstein writes in *The Four Pillars of Investing*, "The stockbroker services his clients in the same way that Bonnie and Clyde serviced banks."

You may find some of these judgments harsh. After all, most brokers and other financial advisors are good people who want to do right by their clients. They realize that a long-term relationship only results from a satisfied client. And, in a perfect world, perhaps both brokers and their customers could be fully satisfied.

Unfortunately, we don't live in a perfect world. There is a fundamental misalignment of interests here. As an investor, you want to earn the highest net returns. Your advisor has a slightly different agenda. He wants you to earn the highest return *net of his fees.* There's an important difference.

Most stockbrokers, for example, are better salespeople than investment advisors. (Or, as my friend Scott Whitmore at Morgan Stanley likes to say, "It's 97% of investment advisors that give the other 3% of us a bad name.) Virtually everyone on Wall Street—naturally—wants to earn as high an income as possible. Unfortunately, that can only be achieved by converting a significant percentage of client assets into their assets. That's how the business works.

This would be perfectly fair if most investment advisors earned higher returns than you could achieve on your own. Alas, this is hardly the case.

LET THE BUYER BEWARE

As I traveled around the country to seminars and conferences after the dot-com crash, I heard a great deal of resentment from ordinary investors. They were angry at mutual fund companies that successfully marketed five-star performance and the notion that their funds could beat the market over the long haul. They told me they were fed up with investment analysts who privately referred to their "strong buy" recommendations as "pigs," "powder kegs," and "pieces of junk." They felt like they had been had by brokers and financial planners whose interest in their own fees and commissions exceeded their interest in their clients' financial welfare. They were tired of insurance agents who tried to sell them more protection than they needed, at prices only the unsophisticated would pay.

They were angry, too, at corrupt corporate chieftains—at companies like Enron, Adelphia, Global Crossing, and WorldCom—who sold employees and shareholders down the river to satisfy their own lust for power and money. And they were painfully aware that leading Wall Street firms had paid the biggest fines in SEC history—a total of more than $1.1 billion—for blatantly compromising their retail clients' interests while courting publicly traded companies for investment banking business.

Eventually, investors woke up to the simple fact that many of these folks were nothing more than self-interested parties whose overriding interest was separating them from their money. This is not always true, as I've said. But aside from ethical considerations, there is the question of competence.

You might think that once a new hire becomes a stockbroker, for instance, his firm will teach him everything he needs to know about how to manage his client's money intelligently. This is emphatically not the case. As author William Bernstein writes, "It is a sad fact that you can pass the Series 7 exam and begin to manage other people's life savings faster than you can get a manicurist's license in most states."

Plus, Wall Street firms give brokers—even brand-spanking-new ones—a great deal of leeway in determining how to invest their client's hard-earned money. Without a lot of personal experience to draw on, this can be a recipe for disaster. Just as a recent college graduate with a business degree is rarely qualified to set up or run his own business, a freshly minted registered representative is unlikely to be the best-qualified person to manage your nest egg.

When I worked in the investment industry, I was astonished to find how little some of my colleagues understood about the financial markets. It took me a while to realize this, in part because when I started, I knew even less than they did. Yet these were my mentors. And the first thing I learned—something that sticks with me to this day—is how expensive (and painful) it is to learn Wall Street's lessons the hard way.

Yet I generally did. For starters, my associates were inveterate market timers. That means they had convinced themselves that they knew when to be in the market for the rallies and out for the corrections (and bear markets). Unlike the vast army of brokers on Wall Street, however, who are forever seeing nothing but blue skies ahead, my early colleagues were forever predicting that the stock market was on the verge of collapse.

When I joined the firm in 1985, the Dow had just crossed the 1,400 mark. In hindsight, this was one of the great buying opportunities of the twentieth century. Although there would be many drops along the way—not least of all, the crash of 1987—the market had 15 years of extraordinary performance just ahead.

Yet our company chairman, who was also the head of "research," regularly warned us that the U.S. market was wildly overvalued and likely to plunge at any time. We were an international investment firm and our outlook for Hong Kong, Australia, Switzerland, and other foreign markets was, conveniently, more sanguine.

Eventually, the U.S. market did crash, along with international exchanges. Thus vindicated, our chairman remained stubbornly bearish throughout the 1990s. Yet this time the market refused to cooperate. Fortunately, it didn't matter to me or my clients. I had long since shrugged off the apocalyptic nonsense about "the coming crash" and began searching for a workable investment strategy.

A TRIO WORTH LISTENING TO

As a subscriber to the *Wall Street Journal* and other mainstream financial publications, I realized that there were a handful of investors whose investment returns were leaving the rest of us on the roadside. These included Peter Lynch, who was managing the

Fidelity Magellan Fund; John Templeton, who was running the Templeton Growth Fund; and Warren Buffett, who was running Berkshire Hathaway.

These men didn't need publicity agents. Their audited track records spoke for themselves. As far as I was concerned, the three of them occupied Mt. Olympus.

I began reading everything about them that I could find. I was anxious to find out how they knew exactly when to get into the market and when to get out. I didn't realize that this had absolutely nothing to do with their investment approach. I was still so naive at this point that, not only did I not know the answers, I wasn't even asking the right questions.

Fortunately, it wasn't difficult to figure out what they were doing. Fidelity Investments was more than happy to send me plenty of information explaining Lynch's investment approach.

The Templeton organization was much the same, only better. It sent me regular updates on the Templeton Growth Fund strategy, as well as tapes of John Templeton himself addressing groups of investors on his market approach.

I remember listening to these tapes in my car again and again. Once, a fellow broker riding with me, clearly uninterested in hearing John Templeton expound on his investment principles, finally asked in frustration, "Hey, man, you got any Jimmy Buffett?"

"I've got some *Warren* Buffett," I answered.

"No," he responded with a sour look. "*Jimmy* Buffett."

"Sorry."

My favorite source of information on Warren Buffett was his annual letter to shareholders. These clear, folksy, easy-to-read letters are chock full of investment insights. It was hard for me to believe that the master himself was laying out the principles of successful investment for anyone to read. Best of all, it was free. All you had to do was call Berkshire and request an annual report. (Today you can access these reports online in a matter of seconds at berkshirehathaway.com.)

These are still some of the best and most accessible writings on value investing. They formed the foundation of much of what

I found useful in the world of investing. And the principles they espouse are timeless.

(There is, however, one small drawback. There is only one Warren Buffet. And if you take a quick look in the mirror, I'll think you'll find that you're not him.)

As I studied the investment principles of these three men, I was surprised to discover that none were market timers. Even though their approaches to buying and selling stocks were very different, they all approached the market with the same general philosophy. And that included a concession that they didn't have the slightest clue whether the market was about to go up or down. Instead, they made their money identifying companies that were trading below their intrinsic worth and selling them when the market recognized that value. (Easier said than done, by the way.)

So even the world's best investors understand you do not gain an edge by trying to time the market. If you remain skeptical on this point, listen to the words of some of the most successful investors of all time:

- Benjamin Graham, the father of value investing: "If I have noticed anything over these 60 years on Wall Street, it is that people do not succeed in forecasting what's going to happen to the stock market."
- Warren Buffett: "We've long felt that the only value of stock forecasters is to make fortune tellers look good. Even now, Charlie [Munger] and I continue to believe that short-term market forecasts are poison and should be kept locked up in a safe place, away from children and also from grown-ups who behave in the market like children."
- John Templeton, pioneer of global investing and legendary manager of the Templeton Growth Fund: "I never ask if the market is going to go up or down next year. I know there is no one who can tell me that."
- Peter Lynch, the best performing mutual fund manager of all time, in his book *One Up on Wall Street*: "Thousands of experts study overbought indicators, oversold indicators, head-and-shoulder patterns, put-call ratios, the Fed's policy on money

supply, foreign investment, the movement of the constellations through the heavens, and the moss on oak trees, and they can't predict the markets with any useful consistency, any more than the gizzard squeezers could tell the Roman emperors when the Huns would attack."

He ends his book by telling readers, "What the market is going to do ought to be irrelevant. If I could convince you of this one thing, I'd feel this book had done its job."

Why doesn't your investment advisor, obviously a smart guy, give up the economic forecasts and market predictions? Vanguard® founder John Bogle put it best when he wrote in *The Little Book of Common Sense Investing*, "It's amazing how difficult it is for a man to understand something if he's paid a small fortune not to understand it."

This message also goes against the instincts—not to mention the hypercharged emotions—of most investors. They want to believe they are smart to move their money around in anticipation of the next big market move. But it boils down to this: You can listen to an investment advisor or stock market guru who has a market timing system to sell. Or you can listen to the greatest investors of all time. The choice is yours.

Your broker or investment advisor is probably expensive. And you may imagine you're getting what you pay for. After all, this line of thinking is true in most walks of life. You want to use the best builder for your home, the best accountant for your business, the best doctor for your surgery. But do you really need the best broker?

No, you don't.

In this industry there is a lot of jargon and investment complexities that are off-putting to the average investor. But you no more need to master all this arcane knowledge to manage your money effectively than you need to understand how a combustion engine works to drive from here to the post office. Successful investing does not have to be terribly complicated. Or as Warren Buffett says, "It is not necessary to do extraordinary things to get extraordinary results."

Simplicity and effectiveness lie at the heart of the Gone Fishin' Portfolio. You won't need an investment advisor to put it together— or to run it.

REEL IT IN...

1. History shows that Wall Street excels at salesmanship, not money management.
2. In most walks of life, you get what you pay for. This is emphatically not the case with most investment advisors.
3. No one cares more about your money than you do. You should manage it yourself.
4. It makes sense to take investment cues from the world's great investors, like Peter Lynch, John Templeton, and Warren Buffett.
5. These three investment icons understand that—whatever your investment approach—you do not gain an edge by trying to time the market.

CHAPTER 4

Know What You Don't Know

"The greatest obstacle to discovery is not ignorance—
it is the illusion of knowledge."

—Daniel J. Boorstin

We live in an uncertain world, especially when it comes to securing our financial well-being. Think about it. The economy expands and contracts. Jobs are created and destroyed. Inflation ebbs and flows. Stocks rise and fall.

And then there is the occasional bolt out of the blue. Companies collapse. Foreign governments fail. Markets crash. Terrorists attack without warning.

It's a bit unnerving for those of us seeking a bit of financial security, and the peace of mind that comes with it.

Fortunately, the Gone Fishin' Portfolio takes life's unavoidable risks and uncertainties and turns them into your ally. It allows you to reach financial independence, not because of how much you know, but, ironically, by conceding how much you don't.

To most investors, this is wildly counterintuitive. After all, we know there is a high correlation between education and income. (The average college graduate, for example, makes almost 70% more per year than workers with just a high school diploma.) So when it comes to investing, it's natural to assume that the smartest investors are the most successful.

That's not necessarily true. Experience shows that more often, it's humility—not superior knowledge—that leads to success in the world of investing.

Albert Einstein, for example, is the universal symbol of genius. He discovered the theory of relativity, won the Nobel Prize in physics, and made scientific advances in gravity, cosmology, radiation, theoretical physics, statistical mechanics, quantum theory, and unified field theory. Wouldn't an investor be blessed to have an IQ like this?

Perhaps not. Einstein lost his investment capital—including his Nobel Prize money—on bonds that defaulted. For all his genius, he was a failure at investing.

Or take Long Term Capital Management (LTCM). LTCM was a hedge fund created in 1994 with the help of two Nobel Prize–winning economists. The fund incorporated a complex mathematical model designed to profit from inefficiencies in world bond prices. The brilliant folks in charge of the fund used a statistical model that they believed eliminated risk from the investment process. And if you've eliminated risk, why not bet large?

So they did, accumulating positions totaling $1.25 trillion. Of course, they hadn't really eliminated risk. And when Russia defaulted on its sovereign debt in 1998, the fund blew up. LTCM shareholders lost $4.6 billion in less than four months. To clean up the resulting mess, Federal Reserve Chairman Alan Greenspan had to orchestrate a buyout by 14 major investment banks.

Another example is Mensa. This society welcomes people from all walks of life, provided their IQ is in the top 2% of the population. But these folks could stand to pick up a copy of *Investing for Dummies*. During a recent 15-year period when the S&P 500 had average annual returns of 15.3%, the Mensa Investment Club's performance averaged returns of just 2.5%.

That isn't just lagging performance. It's more like getting left on the station platform. As Warren Buffett once said, "Investing is not a game where the guy with the 160 IQ beats the guy with the 130 IQ."

Believing that you've got it all figured out, or—just as bad— taking investment advice from someone who thinks he does, is generally a shortcut to disaster, not financial security.

Investment success comes from understanding basic investment principles, putting them to work in an effective strategy, and applying a bit of discipline. This idea is straightforward, but completely alien to most people. They figure that the best investors have uncanny insights about what's in store for the economy, interest rates, the dollar, and the stock market. And, if you don't know, well—heck, you have to guess.

NO, YOU DON'T

You can generate superior returns without divining the future— and without guessing about it, either. You need only understand what part of the investment process is knowable and unchanging, and what factors, such as economic growth or market fluctuations, can never be known in advance.

Using proven investment principles in an uncertain world can provide you with outstanding long-term results. And that's just what the Gone Fishin' Portfolio does. It allows you to generate the returns you need without subscribing to the *Wall Street Journal,* without studying your investment holdings for long hours, and without paying a high-priced financial advisor. If you're like many long-term investors who are interested in financial security but uninterested in devoting time to studying the financial markets, this is all you need.

The Gone Fishin' investment philosophy is based on a deep-seated agnosticism about short-term market fluctuations. I don't know what the market is going to do next month or next year. And I'm not ashamed to admit it. Because nobody else knows, either.

Of course, there are plenty of people on Wall Street—and in the investment media—who make a living by pretending to know or, in some cases, by actually deluding themselves that they know.

But thinking that you've got the investment landscape all figured out is a deadly mindset. Pride isn't one of the seven deadly sins for nothing.

HUMILITY IS THE ONLY TRUE WISDOM

The foundation of the Gone Fishin' Portfolio goes all the way back to 327 B.C., when one of the world's greatest investment books was written. For the record, that was a couple millennia before the founding of the London Stock Exchange. But some wisdom is ageless. That's certainly the case with Plato's *Apology*.

As you may recall, Socrates was on trial for corrupting the youth of Athens. He had done no such thing, of course. What he had done was educate them, teaching them to challenge arguments from authority and question what they believed to be true. In the process, he frustrated and embarrassed many powerful people with his persistent line of questioning, known today as the Socratic method.

It is a form of philosophical inquiry that consists of asking someone what he believes to be true, asking him to justify those beliefs, and then challenging him to justify those premises further.

It can be maddening. Try it on your spouse and you'll quickly learn how difficult it is to rationalize your beliefs. (You may also learn how uncomfortable the living room couch is relative to the bed.)

In Plato's *Apology*, the oracle at Delphi had pronounced Socrates the wisest man in Athens. No one was more astonished—or more disbelieving—than Socrates himself. So he immediately set out to disprove the oracle by finding a wiser man.

He started by examining a politician with a reputation for great wisdom, and the ego to go with it. Not only was the old gentleman unable to validate his beliefs, but he resented Socrates' challenge to his authority.

"So I left him," says Socrates, "saying to myself, as I went away: 'Well, although I do not suppose that either of us knows anything really beautiful and good, I am better off than he is, for he knows nothing, and thinks that he knows; I neither know nor think that I know. In this latter particular, then, I seem to have slightly the advantage of him.' Then I went to another who had still higher pretensions to wisdom, and my conclusion was exactly the same. Whereupon I made another enemy of him, and of many others besides him."

In the end, Socrates discovered he was indeed the wisest man in Athens. Not because of how much he knew, but because he was the only one who understood how much he *didn't know*.

Perhaps nowhere is this lesson in humility more valuable than in the world of investing. In the years I spent working with individual investors, I learned that the majority have a serious roadblock between them and financial independence: their own misconceptions.

Having read mainstream financial magazines, watched Jim Cramer's antics, or talked with their friends and neighbors about "hot stocks," many approach the markets with a poor understanding of basic investment concepts. They often believe that investment success comes by jumping from one winning stock to another, like a jockey leaping from horse to horse in a race. In short, too many investors are both unknowledgeable and overconfident. That's a poisonous mix.

A perfect example is the day-trading mania that gripped thousands of otherwise clear-headed individuals during the great technology stock run-up of the 1990s. Many of these investors sincerely believed that they knew what they were doing. They felt that they had a "system" for beating the market and creating short-term wealth. And, for a while at least, their monthly brokerage statements even confirmed it. But when the bear market showed up—as it always does eventually—they ended up going back to their day jobs. No richer, but perhaps a little wiser.

Buffett was right again. "It's only when the tide goes out that you learn who's been swimming naked."

In my experience, one of the biggest hurdles investors face is their own lack of skepticism—or doubt.

CERTAINTY—A FOOL'S PARADISE

Socrates made two important points. First, he told us to acknowledge our limitations, to face up to our own ignorance on certain matters. But he also admonished us to distinguish between those who speak well and those who speak the truth.

There are thousands of smart, articulate, and highly persuasive men and women who make a comfortable living as financial pundits. Most of them sound highly knowledgeable when discussing financial matters. They seem to have mastered all the minutiae of investing. But do they really know what they don't know? Many of them, I can assure you from my years of experience in the investment industry, do not. Even those who have doubts often feel they have to present an all-knowing image to instill confidence in their clients.

Think about this the next time your advisor suggests that now is the time to buy bonds instead of stocks. Or buy growth funds and sell value. How does he know the timing is right? Just what kind of crystal ball does he have?

The truth is, the economy is too big, too dynamic, and too complex to be predicted with any accuracy. The same is true of the stock and bond markets. The average investor's confidence in his or her own ability—or the advisor's ability—to predict the future is almost always misplaced.

Remember the words of Nobel Laureate Nils Bohr: "Prediction is very difficult, especially about the future."

Clients often expect their financial advisor to offer opinions about what the economy is likely to do and how the stock market is likely to perform in the months ahead. So the advisor, knowing what's expected, generally tries to provide the answers (answers, generally, with fee-based investment solutions attached).

Unfortunately, the world doesn't work this way. Anyone can make a good market call. But no one—and no system—can accurately and consistently forecast the future. This idea makes some investors uncomfortable. But as the French Enlightenment philosopher Voltaire said, "Doubt is not a pleasant condition, but *certainty* is an absurd one."

This is a hard concept for many investors to accept because there are so many brokers, advisors, analysts, newsletter editors, and mass-media publications making predictions that are so confident their opinions sound a lot like dead certainties. These folks are often credible and convincing. History demonstrates, however, that they are also very wrong much of the time.

Ask a market timer to provide an audited track record of past forecasts and you're likely to get nothing more than a glib line or a blank stare. There's a good reason, too. *Money* magazine's senior editor recently wrote about the experience of Philip Tetlock, a psychiatrist and professor at the University of California–Berkley and one of the world's foremost authorities on *experts:*

> Starting in the 1980s, Tetlock surveyed professional know-it-alls, including academics, think tankers and journalists, and asked them to make predictions about future events around the world.
>
> The results, published in his book *Expert Political Judgment*, are pretty humbling. The experts he surveyed did no better with predictions in their field of study than "dilettantes," experts from other fields who were just drawing on their general knowledge. Some, in fact, did significantly worse.
>
> "The moderately attentive reader of good newspapers can do as well as someone who devotes many years of study to predicting whether, say, Chinese growth rates will continue or Japan's Nikkei index is going up," says Tetlock.

Ouch.

One reason the experts get away with dubious results is that we let them. Our craving for predictions seems to be more deeply entrenched than any innate sense of skepticism.

It comes as a surprise to many investors, but even the most experienced economists can't tell you how fast the economy is likely to grow, where interest rates are going, or where the dollar is headed.

The best investors know this. Peter Lynch, the legendary fund manager of the Fidelity Magellan Fund, says, "If you spend 13 minutes per year trying to predict the economy, you have wasted 10 minutes."

The mass media is in on it, too. For example, twice a year the *Wall Street Journal* polls 55 of the nation's economists to see what lies ahead for the economy, interest rates, the dollar, and other economic variables. Most of them get it wrong. Their consensus isn't so hot, either.

It's gotten to the point where even the *Wall Street Journal* staff is having a laugh. Reporter Jesse Eisinger writes, "Pity the poor Wall Street economist. Big staffs, sophisticated models, reams of historical data, degrees from schools known by merely the name of the biggest benefactor, and still they forecast about as well as groundhogs." (Punxsutawney Phil may actually have an edge over most of them.)

History also demonstrates that if your portfolio is being run by a market timer—someone who plans to have you invested during market rallies and out during the selloffs—you are wasting both your time and your money. Unfortunately, time and money are exactly the two ingredients required to reach financial independence. You cannot afford to waste either.

Yet eager to trust someone with their savings, too many investors look for a broker, a money manager, a newsletter editor, or television pundit who can tell them what the future holds.

Consciously or unconsciously, they imagine the investment process works something like this: "First you make an educated guess about what the economy is likely to do. Based on this, you have a hunch about where the market is likely to go. And based on that, you have a theory about what sorts of investments you should be buying."

I could be wrong, but I don't think a theory, that's based on a hunch, that's based on a guess, is the best foundation for your investment portfolio. So how do you reach your financial goals? You start by facing facts—by using a system that doesn't rely on guesses about the economy and the stock market, and, as Socrates tells us, by knowing what you don't know.

This radical skepticism threatened the leaders of Athens more than 2,000 years ago. And it threatens Wall Street's livelihood today (although not enough, if you ask me). This philosophy disputes their most cherished assumption: that if you hire enough smart economists, researchers, and analysts, you'll reap market-beating investment performance.

Not so.

Rather, investment success begins with a strong dose of humility—not just about your own knowledge but, just as importantly, about the knowledge of the so-called experts.

Understand that you're finally on the right track the day you say to yourself, "Since no one can tell me with any certainty what the economy or the stock market is going to do next year, how should I run my portfolio?"

Some would call this a confession of ignorance. In truth, it is the beginning of investment wisdom. Because no matter how much you know, or how well informed your advisor is, the reality is that uncertainty will always be your inseparable companion.

By now, you probably feel I've made this point with a jack-hammer. That's been intentional. Having spent many years with investment clients, I know what they expect from their advisor. They want someone to have an informed viewpoint about interest rates, currencies and commodity prices. They want advice on how best to capitalize on current trends. They want someone to help eliminate all the near-term uncertainties.

When I speak at conferences, I explain that they're asking the impossible, that no one truly knows. Afterwards, they often tell me how much they enjoyed my talk. They tell me how much they learned. And then they ask what I think the market is going to do next.

Sometimes I want to pull my hair out.

I understand how deep this "yearning to know" is. But in order to embrace the Gone Fishin' philosophy, you have to let it go.

Rather than pretending to have answers we don't have, we acknowledge our uncertainty. We deal with it. We capitalize on it.

That's what the Gone Fishin' Portfolio is about. It skips the guesswork and endless analysis—and allows you to focus on the important business of meeting your financial objectives.

REEL IT IN...

1. You don't need to predict the future to generate first-class returns.
2. No one—and no system—can accurately and consistently forecast the economy or the financial markets.
3. Experience tells us that it's humility—not superior knowledge—that paves the way to successful investing.
4. Making investment decisions based on hunches or guesses—whether made by you or an expert—is not intelligent risk taking.
5. The Gone Fishin' investment philosophy is based on the notion that nobody knows what the market is likely to do next. This system doesn't eliminate uncertainty. But it does allow you to capitalize on it.

PART II

Get Wealthy

CHAPTER 5

Common Stocks

The Greatest Wealth-Creating Machine of All Time

"I know of no way of judging the future but by the past."

—Patrick Henry

In 1988, Charles Givens published a bestseller called *Wealth Without Risk*. I can only assume it was about inheritance, because I know no other way of getting wealthy without taking risk. (Even the Florida lottery—one of the world's worst bets with 23-million-to-1 odds—requires that you risk a dollar.)

Let's start with a reality check. Successful money management is about the intelligent management of risk. You can't avoid risk or eliminate it. You have to take it by the horns and deal with it.

Every investment choice entails risk. Even if you're so conservative that you keep all your money in cash investments like T-bills and money market funds—not a terribly good idea, incidentally—you are taking the sizable risk that your purchasing power fails to keep pace with inflation.

Yet, terrified of seeing the value of their investments decline even temporarily, plenty of investors do exactly this. This is understandable at first blush. After all, it's not easy watching your nest egg get scrambled as the stock market spasms in reaction to every piece of bad business news or new government statistic.

But relax. History shows that over the long run, you are well compensated for withstanding the vicissitudes of the market. If, by contrast, you seek stability in your investments first and foremost, your returns are guaranteed to be low. Investments in money market funds and certificates of deposit return very little after taxes and inflation. Over the past 80 years, T-bills have returned an average of only 3.8% per year. Sometimes cash returns are considerably worse. In 2004, for example, the average money market yield in the United States was less than 1%, offering a negative real (after-inflation) return on your money.

Don't get me wrong. If you're saving for a short-term goal like a new car or a down payment on a house, you can't get safer than 30-day T-bills. Unless the American flag is no longer flying over the White House a month from now, your investment is secure. However, over the long haul, this kind of safety comes at a steep price. Paradoxically, a portfolio that takes a conservative approach to market risk is often exposed to a high degree of shortfall risk. (This is the risk that you won't be able to meet your spending requirements in retirement.)

Stocks have given far superior long-term returns. Yet many investors are frightened of them. They view the market as a giant casino (and it often acts that way in the short term). But, over the long term, nothing could be further from the truth.

Stocks are not simply slips of paper with corporate names on them. A share of stock is a fractional interest in a business. When a corporation issues stock, it is offering each purchaser the right to share in the fortunes of the business. Once the initial stock offering is complete, shares are then bought or sold on an exchange.

That's when things get interesting. Stocks move day to day based on news or investor perceptions about inflation, interest rates, economic growth, the dollar, consumer confidence, business conditions, government policies, and other factors.

This can cause a company's share price to fluctuate much more dramatically than the prospects for the underlying business. That's because stock prices are determined "at the margin." Only a small fraction of a company's shareholders are actually selling their shares in the market each day. Yet that tiny fraction determines the value of the entire company—at least temporarily. A sudden imbalance in buy or sell orders can quickly push a stock dramatically higher or lower.

Sometimes these price swings are triggered by a change in the company's fundamentals. But a company's daily share price can rise or fall for reasons that have nothing to do with the outlook for the company, or even the economy. Individual stock prices can be pushed around, for example, by rumors, official buy or sell recommendations by major wire houses, short selling, computerized technical strategies, tax selling, good or bad publicity, insider transactions, fads, takeover speculation, or bad news elsewhere in the sector. Short-term momentum traders often pile on too, creating even more havoc.

For short-term traders, these are issues that must be understood and dealt with. But for long-term investors—like those using the Gone Fishin' Portfolio—daily trading activity can be conveniently ignored.

Why? Because over the long term there is one thing about equities that you can safely take to the bank: Share prices follow earnings. (Earnings, of course, are the net profits of the business.) Look back through history and try to find even a single company that increased its earnings quarter after quarter, year after year, and the stock didn't tag along. Conversely, try to uncover one whose earnings declined year after year and the stock continued to move up. It just doesn't happen.

That's why the father of value investing, Benjamin Graham, famously said of the stock market, "In the short run it's a voting machine, but in the long run it's a weighing machine." Regardless of what the market does next week or next month, you can count on it to acknowledge earnings and reward shareholders over the long haul.

When results are measured over long periods, nothing has rewarded investors better than common stocks. Not cash, not bonds, not real estate, not gold, not collectibles, nothing. That's why I call common stocks "the greatest wealth-creating machine of all time."

HISTORY DOESN'T LIE

Dr. Jeremy Siegel, a professor of finance at The Wharton School of the University of Pennsylvania and author of *Stocks for the Long Run,* has done a thorough historical study of the returns of different types of assets over the past couple hundred years.

What he discovered is dramatic: $1 invested in gold in 1802 was worth $32.84 at the end of 2006. The same dollar invested in T-bills would have grown to $5,061. $1 invested in bonds would be worth $18,235. And $1 invested in common stocks with dividends reinvested—drum roll, please—is worth $12.7 million. (See Figure 5.1.)

The odds are good, of course, that you weren't around a couple hundred years ago. And, unless something truly exciting happens soon in the field of cryogenics, you won't be around 200 years from now, either.

However, it's not necessary to think *that* long term. Start whenever you want and you'll find that when measured in decades the

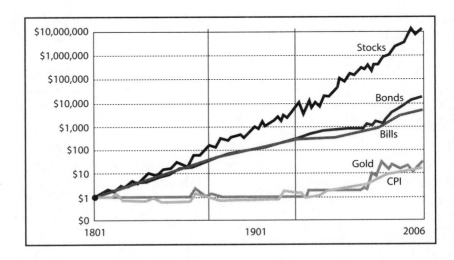

FIGURE 5.1 Total Nominal Return Indices (January 1802 to December 31, 2006)

Source: Jeremy J. Siegel *Stocks for the Long Run,* 4th Ed., McGraw-Hill, 2007.

investment returns for different asset classes are remarkably consistent. Stocks are the big winner. Since 1926, the stock market has generated a positive return in 59 out of 82 calendar years—or nearly three out of every four years.

Of course, it's those inevitable down years that quickly take the fun out of the stock market for most investors. Since 1945, the S&P 500 has tumbled nearly 26%, on average, in the periods leading up to and during recessions.

That often drives investors to the sidelines, where they miss the ensuing rally. Of course, some investors run to bonds or cash when a recession looms. That would be a fine idea, if only recessions were predictable. They're not. Statistics show that recessions tend to be recognized only six to nine months after they begin. By the time headlines confirm that a recession has arrived, the damage in the stock market is usually done.

Of course, even if you somehow knew what was going to happen in the economy, you still wouldn't necessarily know what was going to happen in the stock market. Perversely, stocks often fall during the good times and rally during the bad times. Money manager Ken Fisher doesn't call the stock market "The Great Humiliator" for nothing.

And even if you made a good call and got out of the market before a downturn, how do you know when to get back in? Wait too long and you can miss a substantial part—or all—of the next bull market. That can be costly.

It is clear to anyone who takes the time to investigate that stocks have outperformed all other liquid investments—and illiquid ones, too, including real estate and other tangibles. And while no one can tell you with certainty what investment returns will be in the future, most investors need a fairly high percentage of their portfolio invested in stocks to meet their long-term goals. And they need to stick with this stock market exposure to avoid missing the good times. Never forget that the greatest risk you face as an investor is the possibility that your investments won't last long enough to meet your long-term spending requirements.

Historically, T-bills have returned approximately 3.8% per year. Returns increase with risk: 20-year Treasuries, which come with the same full faith and credit guarantee but can fluctuate widely in value, have returned 5.3%. Large-company stocks have returned 11% per year. And small-company stocks have returned 12%.

These numbers may not mean much to you in the abstract. So let's be more concrete. Using historical averages, if you invested $500 a month into T-bills for 30 years, it turns into $337,853.22. If you invested the same amount into bonds, with interest payments reinvested, it turned into $442,040.56. The same amount invested in stocks, compounded at 11%, turned into more than $1,325,000.

In short, you are well compensated for enduring the constant ups and downs of the stock market. Yes, you're likely to get the sweats from time to time. But when you think about it, whether you're able to meet your spending commitments in retirement is probably more important than what the stock market does this year or next. This is especially true because, while asset returns have been relatively stable over the past couple hundred years, human life spans have changed dramatically.

What does this have to do with your investment strategy?

Everything. The whole point of financial planning is to make sure your investment portfolio doesn't kick the bucket before you do. If you're in good health, you may live a lot longer than you think— or than you're counting on, financially. This means that unless you're independently wealthy—and can live happily ever after with your money tucked away in Triple-A, insured, tax-free bonds—stocks should play an important part in your retirement planning.

This thought scares the bejesus out of novice investors—and a few old hands as well—especially when the market, with no notice whatsoever, begins rumbling like Krakatoa.

This is the norm, however. Investors who expect to earn the generous returns only a diversified stock portfolio can deliver while watching their net worth rise as smoothly as a bank balance are either uninformed or unrealistic. "Steady as she goes," has never described long-term equity investing.

DON'T GET CAUGHT ON THE SIDELINES

Despite the inevitable volatility, there are good reasons to be grateful for the stock market. Capitalism does a better job than any other economic system of creating prosperity. The essence of capitalism is the private ownership of the means of production and distribution. Most of us, however, don't have the capital or the experience to run our own business. (And statistics show that less than half of all new businesses survive their four years.) Enter the stock market, the mechanism that makes capitalism truly democratic.

Even people of modest means can own a stake in a profitable business by investing in stocks. In essence, the stock market allows the little guy to run with the big dogs. Buy a few shares of Microsoft and you'll earn the same return as Bill Gates in the year ahead. Pick up a couple shares of Berkshire Hathaway and your investment will compound at the same rate as Warren Buffett's.

How quickly this notion of owning a profitable business gets lost in the daily headlines, where the focus is constantly shifting from Fed policy to Wall Street downgrades to the latest hedge fund blow-up. Yes, the stock market can be frightening at times. But it is essential that you understand that nothing offers you the prospect of earning higher long-term returns. For this reason, stocks are a key component of the Gone Fishin' Portfolio.

"What about the looming bear market?" some may ask. "Shouldn't we wait until the coast is clear?"

Unfortunately, no one ever signals the "all-clear" in the stock market. At any given time, there are always factors out there that dim the outlook for stocks. If you try to figure out when to be in the market and when to be out, you are engaged in market timing.

This has a seductive allure, I'll agree. After all, when you look backward, it's glaringly obvious when you should have been in the market and when you should have been out. Look forward, however, and it gets a whole lot tougher. All you see is a blank slate.

Market timers often concede their timing won't be perfect, but even missing some of the decline is better than enduring the whole thing, right?

Wrong.

To successfully time the market requires you to buy low, sell high, and then buy low again (while covering all spreads, trading costs, and taxes on capital gains). Fail, and you'll get left behind while the equity train rumbles on.

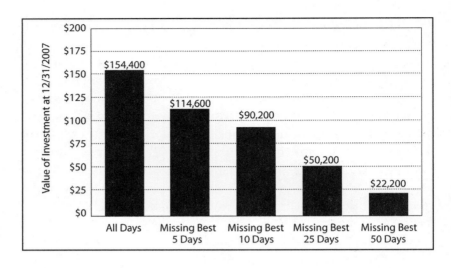

FIGURE 5.2 Hypothetical Growth ($10K invested in the S&P 500 from January 1978 to December 2007)

Note: This example does not include dividend reinvestment or tax implications.

Looking back at the performance of the S&P 500 between 1980 and 2006, if you had missed only the five best-performing days in the market you would have ended up with a portfolio worth 26% less than one that was fully invested throughout the period. As you can see from Figure 5.2, missing only a handful of the market's best-performing days can be costly.

Even more surprising, missing the 30 best days since 1980 would have reduced the value of your portfolio by 73%, compared to one that remained fully invested over the period. Clearly, attempting to move in and out of the market to catch the best possible returns can easily derail your investment plans.

Of course, bearish commentators, some of whom have held the same negative outlook on stocks, not just for years but decades, will argue that the coming market decline will be so painful that you'd better off getting out altogether.

Ironically, these "perma-bears" make a living telling you to sell the very securities that they never recommended you buy in the first place. As for them telling you when to get back in the market, I'll let you in on a little secret: That day never comes.

If you're wondering whether your bearish advisor is a real dyed-in-the-wool grizzly, see if he isn't suggesting your money should be primarily invested in gold. (This sounds suspiciously similar to the "investment" advice my wife gets at the jewelers.) And, while gold bullion does move sharply higher from time to time, as it has in recent years, these moves are largely unpredictable. Furthermore, gold—as you'll see in a moment—has been a poor performer not just over the past few decades, but for centuries.

Perma-bears don't give up easily, though. For those who remain skeptical of their arguments, they aren't afraid to pull out their trump card, the Great Depression.

A REASON FOR OPTIMISM

The Great Depression occurred when the United States and other developed economies were on the gold standard. This greatly restricted the government's ability to respond in the face of an economic crisis. A paper money standard, properly managed, can prevent the severe depressions that plagued the gold standard, while keeping inflation moderate, as we've seen over the past couple of decades.

Still, every stock investor should understand the Great Depression and how it affected investors. For example, in all four editions of *Stocks for the Long Run,* Dr. Jeremy Siegel has told the infamous story of John Jacob Raskob.

In the summer of 1929, *Ladies Home Journal* interviewed Raskob, a senior executive with General Motors, about how the typical individual could build wealth by investing in stocks. In the article published that August, titled "Everybody Ought to Be Rich," Raskob claimed that by putting $15 a month into high-quality stocks, even the average worker could become wealthy.

His timing left something to be desired. Just seven weeks after the article appeared came Black Friday, the stock market crash of 1929. And it wasn't until July 8, 1932, that the carnage finally came to an end. By then, the market value of the greatest corporations in America had declined an astonishing 89%. Millions of investors were wiped out. Thousands who had bought stock on margin (with borrowed money) went bankrupt.

Raskob was held up as an object of ridicule—not only then, but by the gloom-and-doomers of today.

Only . . . what would have happened if you had actually listened to Raskob? Dr. Siegel points out that had you followed Raskob's advice, patiently putting $15 a month in stocks beginning in August 1929 (the equivalent of roughly $220 today), within just four years you would have earned more than someone who put an identical amount in T-bills over the same period. That's right—after just four years, during the worst period of stock market performance in U.S. history.

After 30 years, your portfolio would have grown to $60,000, the equivalent of $313,000 today. That's a 13% annual return, far more than investors would have earned had they switched into T-bills, bonds or gold at the very top of the market.

Some might argue this was a fluke. So let's take a look at another extreme scenario: Germany and Japan after WWII. As Dr. Siegel writes:

> In the 12 years from 1948 to 1960, German stocks rose by over 30% per year in real terms. Indeed, from 1939, when the Germans began the war in Poland, through 1960, the real return on German stocks matched those in the United States and exceeded those in the U.K. Despite the total devastation that the war visited on Germany, the long-run investor made out as well in defeated Germany as in victorious Britain or the United States. The data powerfully attest to the resilience of stocks in the face of seemingly destructive political, social, and economic change. [First Edition, p. 22]

The story in Japan was similar. By the end of 1945, stock prices stood at about approximately a third of their level just prior to the Empire's surrender. Over the next 40 years, the Japanese market returned more than 20 times its American counterpart.

Often, the very best periods of stock market performance come during periods of negative sentiment and high volatility. In fact,

TABLE 5.1 Investing in Stocks During Troubled Times

Date	Subsequent 5-Yr Return	Coincident Event
1932	194%	Great Depression
1982	183%	Worst Recession in Past 25 Years
1994	213%	Dramatic Tightening of Interest Rates

the best five-year return in the U.S. stock market began in May 1932—in the midst of the Great Depression—when stocks returned 367%. The next best five-year period began in July 1982, during one of the worst recessions in the postwar period. As you can see in Table 5.1, it has paid off to stay invested in U.S. stocks during troubled times.

The lesson is this: Over the long haul, stocks have consistently delivered superior returns, throughout expansion, recession, inflation, deflation, and war. Waiting until the backdrop feels "safe" has not been a good method of achieving high future returns.

Of course, the market can always go lower than you think it will—and for longer than you think it will—before a major uptrend appears. For this reason alone, you should not have money invested in stocks that you need in less than five years.

But for your serious, long-term money, there are good reasons to maintain a significant exposure to high-quality stocks. Yes, the stock market will be unnerving and unpredictable in the near term. But inflation makes your future financial requirements unpredictable, too. That's why you need to generate the high returns that only equities can give.

When Siegel's book first came out, detailing the returns of various asset classes, it caused a bit of a sensation. Not because he pointed out that stocks have given the best historical returns. That was already common knowledge, at least among students of the market.

The real barnburner was the following statement from the first edition, based on a thorough examination of two centuries of financial data: "Although bonds are certainly safer than stocks in the short run, over the long run the returns on stocks are so stable that stocks are actually safer than either government bonds or Treasury bills. The constancy of the long-term, after-inflation returns on stocks was truly astounding, while the returns on fixed-income assets posed higher risks for the long-term investor."

Stocks are safer than T-bills? To many investors, that sounds like lunacy. But it has been the case for more than two centuries now. Is it likely to remain so in the future? It is safe to assume so. Let me explain why, not in financial terms but in human ones.

USING THE PAST TO SAFEGUARD YOUR FUTURE

We all have economic needs: food, clothing, shelter, utilities, health care, and so on. It is business—not government—that fills those needs. As long as there are human beings, businesses will prosper by filling those needs. Many investors would benefit from thinking not about the stock market, but about the advantages of owning a portfolio of thriving, profitable businesses. This is likely to remain the most assured route to financial independence.

Of course, any academic can tell you how much stocks have returned in the past. No one can tell you exactly what they will return in the future. But when estimating future returns, it is reasonable to expect that they will not be significantly higher or lower than long-term historical returns.

History clearly demonstrates that no other asset class returns more than stocks over the long haul. Once you understand this—and accept the steep odds against timing the market—you've made the first step toward adopting an investment strategy that can generate high returns within an acceptable level of risk.

Given equities' superior long-term results, a few bold investors may ask, "Why not invest 100% of my portfolio in stocks?"

The answer is human psychology. People are not unfeeling automatons. You have to consider the likelihood that you will stay the course after you've set up a workable strategy. My years as an investment advisor clearly demonstrated to me that most investors have a low pain threshold when it comes to tolerating market declines.

Many felt an overwhelming urge to "do something." And that something was invariably to *sell!* when most of the damage was already done. It was disheartening. However, there are ways to reduce the volatility of your portfolio—and thus your propensity to panic—and still assure high returns.

In fact, that is just the subject we will turn to next.

REEL IT IN...

1. Shortfall risk—the risk of outliving your money—is the biggest threat to your long-term financial security, not stock market fluctuations.
2. The investment that has given the best long-term returns after inflation is common stocks. They should make up the core of your long-term portfolio.
3. It isn't possible to know in advance the best times to be in the market. For this reason, you need to maintain a consistent long-term exposure to equities.
4. The trade-off for investing in stocks is greater volatility than bonds or bills. However, there are ways to reduce this risk, as we discuss in the next chapter.

CHAPTER 6

Don't Buy What Wall Street Is Selling

"The most costly of follies is to believe in the palpably not true."

—H.L. Mencken

History clearly demonstrates that common stocks should provide the foundation of any portfolio designed to maximize total returns. The first question, of course, is how many stocks you should own, and which ones. For the Gone Fishin' strategy, the answer is simple: all of them. We're going to capture the performance of virtually every major company on the world's leading stock exchanges.

This may come as a surprise to my regular readers. After all, I spend several hundred hours a year researching, recommending, and monitoring just a few dozen individual stocks. And not without some success. There are hundreds of investment letters published in the United States. In both 2006 and 2007, the independent *Hulbert Financial Digest* ranked the *Oxford Club Communique,* which I direct, among the top five investment letters in the nation for risk-adjusted returns over the previous five years. (This ranking is due, in part, to the success of my individual stock picks. However, Hulbert also monitors the performance of the Gone Fishin' Portfolio, which has returned 17.3% annually since its inception in 2003 through 2007.)

Why no individual stocks in the Gone Fishin' Portfolio? This strategy is about investing, not trading. It's about meeting long-term goals, not pursuing short-term gains. It's also about spending as little time as possible on your investments, and getting on with your life.

So for this strategy we're going to skip buying and selling individual stocks, which requires a lot of time, attention, and legwork, and own mutual funds instead.

THE MUTUAL FUND ADVANTAGE

More than half of American households now own mutual funds. Most investors are already familiar with them. As you may know, they offer several important advantages:

1. *Diversification.* The risk of owning a whole portfolio of stocks is considerably less than the risk of holding any one of the individual stocks in it. But it can take quite a bit of money to build a diversified portfolio of stocks or bonds. You get instant diversification with each mutual-fund share.

2. *Professional management.* Whether you own an index fund or an actively managed fund, there is a professional manager overseeing the portfolio.

3. *Low minimums.* Each fund establishes its own investment minimum. Each fund in the Gone Fishin' Portfolio has an investment minimum of $3,000. (Small investors can use another alternative I'll describe in Chapter 11.)

4. *No financial advisor required.* You can buy mutual funds that charge no loads (commissions) directly from the fund companies.

5. *Liquidity.* Mutual fund companies will allow you to redeem (sell) all or part of your shares on any day the market is open for trading.

6. *Automatic reinvestment.* You can arrange for all your fund's dividends and capital gains to be automatically reinvested in the fund—or directed to other funds—without charge.

7. *Convenience.* You can buy and redeem most fund shares online, by phone, or by mail. You can arrange automatic purchases from your bank account. Or you can arrange regular periodic withdrawals. You can also arrange that the proceeds from your funds' redemptions or distributions be deposited in your bank account.

8. *Simplified record keeping.* You will receive regular statements showing the value of your account and any activity. At the end of each year, you'll receive the tax-reporting information you need, too.

9. *Customer service.* If you have a question or a problem, or need to make changes to your account, you can call your fund's toll-free customer service line and get the help you need at no additional cost.

10. *Time.* Owning shares of a mutual fund saves you the trouble of researching, constructing, and monitoring a portfolio of individual stocks.

THE WISER BET

There are essentially two types of mutual funds: index funds and actively managed funds:

1. *Index funds.* With indexing, the fund manager attempts to replicate the return of a particular benchmark, such as the S&P 500 or the Lehman Brothers Aggregate Bond Index. Index fund managers generally do not buy stocks or bonds that are not included in the benchmark.

2. *Actively managed funds.* Active managers try to outperform the benchmark by selecting the best-performing securities or trying to time the market.

Some readers may question why any investor would settle for the performance of an index when you can use a fund manager who is willing to swing for the fences. After all, people like Peter Lynch,

John Templeton, and Bill Miller have become household names by beating the indexes soundly.

However, you may not realize just how exceptional—and rare—these men are. Investing in actively managed funds is generally an exercise in futility. That's because the overwhelming majority of actively managed funds fail to beat their benchmark.

Need proof? There's plenty of it. In 1967, for example, academic Michael Jensen decided to evaluate mutual fund managers, testing for evidence of the ability to consistently beat the stock market averages. What he discovered—and scores of studies have subsequently confirmed—is that the average fund produces roughly the same gross return as the market. Unfortunately, the average investor receives a *net* return equal to the market's less expenses. As you'll see, these expenses add up quickly, dramatically reducing the final value of your portfolio. Expenses alone keep most actively managed funds powerless to keep pace with index funds.

In *What Wall Street Doesn't Want You to Know*, Larry E. Swedroe cites a more recent study. He writes that, "Mark Carhart conducted the most comprehensive study ever done on the mutual fund industry. He found that once you account for style factors (small-cap vs. large-cap and value vs. growth) the average actively-managed fund underperformed its benchmark by almost 2% per annum." That's nearly 20% of the market's long-term return.

Similarly, research done by James L. Dais and reported in *Financial Analysts Journal* in 2001 concluded, "The results of this study are not good news for investors who purchase actively managed mutual funds. No investment style generates positive abnormal returns over the 1965–1998 sample period. The sample includes 4,686 funds covering 26,564 fund-years."

Of course, some financial advisors simply shrug and tell you, "Don't buy the average funds. Buy the good ones." But there's the rub. Studies show that a fund that beats the market one year is no more likely than its competitors to outperform it the following year.

In *The Little Book of Common Sense Investing*, Vanguard founder John Bogle quotes David Swenson, chief investment officer of the Yale University Endowment Fund: "A miniscule 4% of funds produce market-beating after-tax results with a scant 0.6% (annual) margin of gain. The 96% of funds that fail to meet or beat the

Vanguard 500 Index Fund lose by a wealth-destroying margin of 4.8% per annum."

When the fund industry prints its famous disclaimer, "Past performance is no guarantee of future results," it isn't just whistling "Dixie." Past is not prologue when it comes to the performance of the best actively managed funds. That's why it's estimated that over half of all institutional monies are now invested using indexing strategies.

In an earlier chapter, I quoted top-performing investment managers like Warren Buffett and Peter Lynch. Yet even they agree with the power of indexing. In the April 2, 1990, issue of *Barron's,* Peter Lynch said, "[Most investors would] be better off in an index fund." In his 1996 letter to Berkshire Hathaway, Warren Buffett said, "The best way to own common stocks is through an index fund . . ."

The question you should ask yourself is, "If the nation's most sophisticated institutions are using an indexing strategy, should I be, too?" The answer is an unequivocal yes. Actively managed funds are laden with higher management and administrative fees. These funds may also charge front-end or back-end loads and 12b-1 fees— expenses that will make your head spin. There are other costs, too. And oftentimes they are not itemized neatly for you. Instead, the specifics are often buried in fine print in the prospectus.

Of course, selecting the so-called "best performing" funds may be the way your broker or financial advisor makes a living. But the sooner you realize these funds are unlikely to outperform their benchmarks, the quicker you'll be on your way to securing your financial freedom. It's a straightforward equation, really. The fees you pay directly reduce your investment portfolio's returns. More money in expenses means less money in your pocket. It's that simple.

THE LOW-FEE WAY TO BEAT THE STREET

Arthur Levitt, the longest-serving chairman of the Securities and Exchange Commission (SEC), published a business bestseller exposing Wall Street's agenda, *Take On the Street: What Wall Street and Corporate America Don't Want You to Know.*

In it, he declares:

> Investors today are being fed lies and distortions, are being exploited and neglected. In the wake of the last decade's rush to invest by millions of households, a culture of gamesmanship has grown among corporate management, financial analysts, brokers, and fund managers, making it hard to tell financial fantasy from reality.

If this all sounds a bit depressing, cheer up. The Gone Fishin' Portfolio offers an effective solution. The portfolio consists entirely of low-cost Vanguard funds that charge no loads and no 12b-1 fees. Vanguard's fees are the lowest in the mutual fund industry.

I could have chosen almost any fund group to run the Gone Fishin' Portfolio. However, the Vanguard Group is special. It is among the nation's largest mutual fund groups with more than $1.1 trillion in assets under management. Such a large asset base allows the company to enjoy economies of scale that allow it to maintain its position as the lowest-cost fund family in the industry.

Plus, its structure is unique. The Vanguard Group is owned entirely by its individual funds, and, ultimately, the shareholders. It operates the funds "at cost"—charging only the amounts needed to cover operating costs and extracting no profits. That means no fund family is likely to seriously challenge Vanguard's low-cost leadership.

Vanguard also embodies a particular philosophy of investing, one that, in many respects, dovetails nicely with our Gone Fishin' Portfolio. The story of this fund family and its founder John Bogle is one worth telling.

In 1949, Bogle was a graduate student at Princeton University who needed a topic for his thesis. He stumbled on an article in *Fortune* magazine about the mutual fund industry, an industry so small and young at the time that Bogle had never heard of it. Since no academics had researched or published on the topic, Bogle decided to lead the way. And lead he did.

Bogle earned an A+ on his thesis, "The Economic Role of the Investment Company." It included a number of revelations that would change the face of personal investing. He pointed out that the vast majority of mutual fund managers did not beat the market with any consistency. (A reality—as we've seen—that has not changed over the last 60 years.) In fact, most performed worse than a random sample. He also found that mutual fund fees were too high, especially the front-end sales loads. Some investors may ask "Why didn't the fund family lower them to increase investor returns?"

Wise up. That's not how the mutual fund business works.

Bogle showed that lowering the loads led to a loss of interest from salespeople and resulted in lost business for the fund companies. He further concluded that a perfect fund, one with the benefits of the shareholder in mind, would follow an index and charge the lowest fees possible. This would provide a higher long-term net return to the shareholder. This, as we now know, was a revolutionary idea.

A job offer based on the strength of his thesis soon followed. Bogle went to work at Wellington Management Company straight out of college, and was running the company by age 36. He was let go after the early 1970s market crash. Nine months later, however, he founded a fund company based on his own investment principles. The Vanguard Group was born.

It's worth noting that John Bogle wrote up his discoveries in 1951. Yet for 25 years, no one started an index fund. Today, the mutual fund industry is enormous. In 2006, U.S. mutual funds had $10.4 trillion in assets under management. That same year, investors plowed $227 billion into broker-sold funds with loads. Only $166 billion came from investors wise enough to invest in no-load funds. This was no anomaly. Broker-sold stock and bond funds regularly attract more money than lower-cost no-load funds.

LOWER COSTS/HIGHER RETURNS

Bogle has devoted his career to steering investors in the right direction, arguing that, "The central principle of the mutual fund business should be, not the marketing of financial products to customers, but the stewardship of investment services for clients." To Bogle, stewardship doesn't mean just charging more competitive fees. It means delivering higher returns by charging the lowest fees possible. It means not deceiving clients with hyperbolic marketing claims. Most importantly, it means putting the interests of shareholders first.

Vanguard fees are approximately one-fourth of the industry average. According to Morningstar, Table 6.1 shows the annual expenses charged by Vanguard funds compared to the average fund in each asset class.

This analysis actually understates the difference between Vanguard fund fees and ordinary fund fees. That's because with actively managed funds, there are actually three more layers of expenses beyond the fund's expense ratio listed in the prospectus and annual reports.

The expense ratio merely comprises administrative expenses plus management fees. But actively managed funds incur many other costs that shareholders ultimately bear.

For example, funds must pay commissions on transactions. With actively managed funds, these can be substantial. As an individual investor, you can enter an online order with your discount broker and pay less than $10 to have them execute it. But things aren't so simple in the fund industry. Funds need specialists to handle the large transactions that they make. And even the best-informed investors generally don't know their funds' trading costs. That's because, while the SEC requires that they be reported to shareholders, the presentation is generally so obscure that you're unlikely to find them unless you're a CPA.

TABLE 6.1 Vanguard's Fees vs. Industry Average

Fund	Vanguard Fee	Average Fee
Small Cap Index	0.23%	1.43%
Emerging Markets Index	0.37%	2.01%
European Stock Index	0.22%	1.78%
Short-Term Bond Index	0.18%	1.00%
REIT Index	0.20%	1.54%
Inflation Protected Securities Fund	0.20%	1.02%
Pacific Stock Index	0.22%	1.70%
Total Stock Market Index	0.15%	1.18%
High Yield Corp Bond Fund	0.26%	1.24%
Vanguard Precious Metals and Mining Fund	0.28%	1.64%

Another cost fund shareholders must absorb is the bid–ask spread on each security. A stock is always offered slightly higher than it is bid. This spread can be as much as 0.5% even for blue chip stocks. For small-cap stocks, it may be 2% or more. And spreads for foreign stocks can be 5% or more, especially in emerging markets. Clearly, a fund that is trading actively has high hurdles to clear.

Yet another cost to shareholders is what is known as *market-impact* cost. This is not reported and difficult to estimate. Impact costs arise when large blocks of stock are bought or sold by institutional investors, like pension plans, hedge funds, and mutual funds. Bear in mind, if you're a manager running hundreds of millions or billions of dollars in client assets, you can't simply click a mouse and liquidate your holdings at the market. Such a huge sell order would temporarily wreck the price of the security you're trying to sell, reducing shareholders' returns. The same is true if you're accumulating a position in a stock. You would bid up the price of the securities as you bought them. Typically, a fund manager needs days or weeks to accumulate or unwind a position. Who gets stuck with the market-impact cost? Go look in the mirror.

A NEEDLESS DRAG ON PERFORMANCE

This mountain of costs is unrecognized by most fund investors. They are also substantial. In *The Intelligent Asset Allocator,* William Bernstein estimates that the expense ratio, commissions, bid–ask spreads, and impact costs of actively managed funds total 2.2% for large-cap funds, 4.1% for small cap and foreign funds, and a whopping 9% for emerging-market funds. These costs are a serious drag on performance and yet another reason to favor index funds over actively managed funds.

Especially since Vanguard's costs are going down, not up. "Since the beginning of the decade, the average expense ratio of Vanguard funds has declined by nearly 30%," writes Chairman John Brennan, "resulting in savings to our clients of roughly $1 billion in 2006."

Clearly, you have an enormous cost advantage using Vanguard. This is no industry secret, by the way. Vanguard has been named

"Best Buy" by *Forbes* magazine, "Best Service" by *Mutual Fund Magazine,* "Best Fund Family" and "Best Discount Broker" by *Worth* and also "Best Fund Family" by *Smart Money.*

With Vanguard, you know exactly what you're getting. Vanguard stock and bond funds stay fully invested in their target markets. Their managers do not try to time the market. Vanguard does not advertise its funds' past returns or peer rankings, which are based on past performance and can mislead investors.

In short, the interests of Vanguard shareholders and fund managers are completely aligned. That means lower fees, less hassles, no sales pressure, and higher net returns. That's why the Vanguard Group is the best mutual fund family for constructing The Gone Fishin' Portfolio that I'm about to unveil. However, when speaking at conferences about this portfolio, I often have investors tell me something like, "The bulk of my money is in my 401(k). And my 401(k) plan doesn't offer Vanguard funds. What should I do?"

401(k) plans are great for encouraging saving and investment. But the downside may be a lack of flexibility. It may offer a limited number of investment choices determined by your plan provider. You may or may not have a choice of investing in Vanguard funds. If Vanguard is available, by all means take advantage of it. If not, you can substitute other no-load funds based on the asset allocation model in Figure 7.1 on page 81 and achieve much the same results.

If you have any reservations about relying on index funds rather than using an active manager, heed the words of Douglas Dial, a portfolio manager of the CREF Stock Account Fund, the largest pool of equity money in the world.

Dial is a former active manager who has had a conversion. "Indexing is a marvelous technique. I wasn't a true believer. I was just an ignoramus. Now I am a convert. Indexing is an extraordinarily sophisticated thing to do . . . If people want excitement, they should got to the racetrack or play the lottery."

Why don't you read more about this in the mass media? You do, occasionally. But the overriding goal at *Forbes, Fortune, Smart Money, BusinessWeek* and similar publications is not to make readers rich. Their goal is to sell subscriptions, rent lists, and sell advertising. Actively managed funds and brokerage firms are among their largest advertisers. Why alienate them? And how can you devote space to a complete investment strategy like this one every month, when the goal is to keep potential readers tantalized with dreams of ever-new ways of getting rich?

Sadly, few stand to profit from laying out the truth. Not brokerage firms. Not the mutual fund industry. Not the mass media. Everyone has an agenda, it seems. You, however, should have an agenda of your own. And that is shutting out the noise and confusion created by Wall Street's marketing machine so you can take effective responsibility for your financial security.

As I'll describe in the next chapter, the Gone Fishin' Portfolio gives you all the tools you need.

REEL IT IN...

1. The easiest and most convenient way to own common stocks is through mutual funds. They offer diversification, professional management, low minimums, automatic reinvestment, and other conveniences.
2. Index funds are preferable to actively managed funds. Over time, they are likely to deliver higher net returns to shareholders.
3. The Vanguard Group is one of the nation's largest fund groups. Its size and unique structure allows it to offer mutual fund investors the lowest costs in the industry.
4. For these, and other advantages I'll soon discuss, your first choice should be to construct the Gone Fishin' Portfolio using Vanguard Funds.

CHAPTER 7

Your Single Most Important Investment Decision

"Make everything as simple as possible, but not simpler."

—Albert Einstein

The Gone Fishin' Portfolio has two objectives. One is to help you earn a higher return within an acceptable level of risk. The other is to save you time and simplify your life.

However, the investment community and financial press spew out so much analysis and so many opinions each week, it's possible to lose sight of the big picture.

This is particularly true with the rise of so much financial journalism on TV. Turn on CNBC or MSNBC and you're likely to see every major earnings release scrutinized, every piece of pending legislation examined with an eye toward how investors should react.

If you are a short-term trader, there is often news that you should understand and respond to. But for the long-term investor, the day-to-day noise can be conveniently ignored.

A few years ago, for example, a major television station called my office and asked if I would appear on its news show to recommend the steps investors should take in the wake of Hurricane Katrina. My publisher thought it would provide valuable exposure for our organization and encouraged me to do it. I refused.

True, Katrina caused a real mess. But the hurricane had come and gone. Damage to commercial properties and oil refineries was already reflected in share prices—and in some cases was made before Katrina even made landfall.

To go on national TV and suggest that investors should now begin rearranging their portfolios made no sense. (Of course, the station had no problem finding another commentator eager to fill in.)

Long-term investors are better off watching reruns than listening to all the talking heads on the investment shows. At least *The Beverly Hillbillies* won't persuade you to abandon your investment discipline.

SIX CRUCIAL FACTORS

Let's get past this week's money supply figures and today's advance/decline ratio and get down to brass tacks. There are only six factors that determine the long-term value of your investment portfolio:

1. How much you save
2. How long your investments compound
3. Your asset allocation
4. Those assets' annual return
5. How much you pay in annual expenses
6. How much you pay in taxes

That's it. Whether you're investing $10,000 or $10 million, these six factors will determine what your net worth eventually becomes. So let's take a closer look at each.

How Much You Save

I've already devoted a chapter to saving and told you it's important to save as much as you can, as soon as you can, for as long as you can. Understand, too, that it's tremendously beneficial to keep saving even as your portfolio takes wing.

For example, let's say you've accumulated a portfolio worth $100,000. If it compounds at no more than the long-term return of the S&P 500—11% a year—it will be worth $1,358,000 in 25 years. Not bad. But if you add $500 a month along the way, it will grow to more than $2.1 million.

Realize that you can have the world's most sophisticated investment strategy, but if you've only saved a pittance, it won't make much difference. Before you can invest seriously, it is essential to forgo spending.

It's also important to save in a qualified retirement plan first, where your money compounds tax-deferred and your contribution may be tax deductible. This is especially true if you contribute to an employer-sponsored plan that provides matching benefits.

How Long Your Investments Compound

There are two ways to let your investments compound longer. You can start investing sooner or you can keep working longer. Or both. If you're 20 years old, for example, you need only have $31,326.88 compound at 8% to accumulate $1 million at age 65. But to fully appreciate the high cost of waiting, look at Table 7.1. At 40, you need to have $146,017.90 compounding at 8% to reach $1 million by age 65. At 55, the number turns into $463,193.49. Clearly, it's in your interest to let money start compounding as soon as you can—and leave it alone as long as you can.

This requires more than a little discipline. But it's imperative that you adopt a hand's-off mentality toward your investments. You can't enjoy the benefits of compounding if you interrupt the process by tapping your portfolio from time to time to buy a new car, remodel the kitchen, or take that trip to Lake Tahoe you've been dreaming about. (If you must have these things, save for them separately.)

TABLE 7.1 Amount Needed at 8% Annual Return to Reach $1 Million at 65

Age	Investment
15	$21,321.23
20	$31,327.88
25	$46,030.93
30	$67,634.54
35	$99,377.33
40	$146,017.90
45	$214,548.21
50	$315,241.70
55	$463,193.49
60	$680,583.20

Source: The Bogleshead's Guide to Investing. (John Wiley & Sons, 2006).

Albert Einstein famously said that the most powerful force in the universe is money compounding. Let the force be with you.

Your Asset Allocation

Investors are often surprised to learn that their most important investment decision is selecting the mix of assets to be held in the portfolio, not selecting the individual investments themselves. This is asset allocation. It's how you divide your portfolio up among different uncorrelated assets like stocks and bonds. (By uncorrelated, I mean they don't necessarily move in the same direction at the same time.) As we've seen, stocks give the greatest return over the long haul. The trade-off is high volatility. Blending different types of stocks with other assets can generate excellent returns with less risk than being fully invested in stocks (more on this important topic in a moment).

How Much Your Investments Return Annually

This is the great unknown, of course. Outside of low-returning, risk-free assets, you cannot know with any certainty what your returns will be in the year ahead. But over the long haul, the returns on various asset classes are remarkably stable. Our goal with the Gone

Fishin' Portfolio is to generate higher than average returns while keeping risk carefully controlled.

How Much You Pay in Annual Expenses

All things being equal, the higher your investment costs, the lower your annual returns, and the longer it will take you to reach your financial goals. Keeping investment expenses to a minimum is crucial, although I can guarantee it's not your investment advisor's biggest priority. Sure, he wants you to earn good returns. But he may have his eye on that new BMW 7 Series, too.

How Much You Pay in Taxes

I don't care how patriotic you are, when financial independence is your goal, the IRS is not your friend. The taxman can take good returns and reduce them to mediocre returns very quickly. Yet many investors fail to consider the tax consequences of their actions. Many needlessly fork over thousands of dollars each year by failing to "tax-manage" their investments. Doing this requires you to take a few steps to minimize the annual tax bite to your portfolio. (This is an important topic that I'll cover in more detail in Chapter 10.)

IMPORTANCE OF THESE FACTORS IN THE GONE FISHIN' PORTFOLIO

Please appreciate that these six crucial factors will determine both the long-term value of your portfolio and your quality of life in retirement. So they loom large in our Gone Fishin' Portfolio.

Note, too, that of these six essential factors, only one is beyond your control. Which one? Number 4. No matter how proficient you are as an investor, you cannot control your portfolio's annual investment returns. Yet this is the factor so many investors spend their time fretting about. What is the stock market going to do? When will my bonds bounce back? Are gold stocks finally set to rally? You might as well ask what the weather will be like six weeks from Saturday. Nobody knows.

The Gone Fishin' Portfolio eliminates the perpetual guessing game about what lies ahead for the economy and the markets. Instead, you accept what you don't know (and can't control) and focus on those things you do know and can control—specifically, saving, compounding, asset allocation, costs and taxes.

Of these five factors we can control, the most important is your asset allocation. It is your single most important investment decision. I realize that's a bold claim, so let me provide the evidence.

In the 1980s, Gary Brinson, a noted money manager and financial analyst, published two sophisticated studies in *Financial Analysts Journal,* analyzing the returns of pension fund managers. They clearly demonstrated that—over the long term—asset allocation accounted for over 90% of the total return of a diversified investment portfolio. The rest was due to other factors, including security selection and market timing.

These results—which have been confirmed by many other studies—are startling. It means that over the long term, your chosen asset allocation is 10 times as important as security selection and market timing combined.

HIGHER RETURNS WITH LESS VOLATILITY

The goal of asset allocation is to create a diversified portfolio with the highest possible return within an acceptable level of risk. You achieve this by combining noncorrelated assets, like stocks, bonds, and real estate investment trusts (REITs). Academics call it building an *efficient portfolio.*

When I talk to investors about asset allocation, they are often dismissive. "Oh, I understand asset allocation," many of them say. "That means you should diversify. I do that already."

But asset allocation is more than simple diversification. If you own an S&P 500 index fund, for example, you are broadly diversified. (After all, you own a piece of 500 different companies.) But you aren't properly asset allocated, because the S&P 500 only gives you exposure to U.S. large-cap stocks.

Other investors tell me they don't even have an asset allocation. They do. Everyone does. Even if all your money is in Treasury bills, you have an asset allocation. It's not a particularly good one, however. It's 100% cash.

As we've discussed, U.S. stocks have historically returned a little more than 10% annually; bonds, roughly 6%, and money markets, about 4%. Over time, your portfolio will be driven by the return of these asset classes. So, for example, a portfolio with 80% of its assets in bonds and 20% in stocks will behave very differently than one with 80% in stocks and 20% in bonds. Over time, the latter portfolio is likely to generate far superior results.

In my experience, most investors have only a vague notion what their asset allocation is. To determine yours, simply total up the value of all your liquid assets—stocks, bonds, mutual funds, and bank accounts—and then determine what percentage of your total portfolio is in stocks, what percentage is in bonds and what percentage is in cash. Those percentages make up your basic asset allocation.

(If you are uncertain which asset classes the funds you own fall in, contact the funds themselves. They'll be happy to tell you.)

THE GONE FISHIN' ASSET ALLOCATION MODEL

In essence, the Gone Fishin' Portfolio is an asset allocation model. Its goal is to match or exceed the return of being fully invested in stocks without enduring the hair-raising volatility of a 100% stock portfolio. In the five years since I created it, it has done just that, returning 17.3% a year while experiencing less volatility than the S&P 500.

The Gone Fishin' Portfolio is made up of 10 Vanguard mutual funds. Although I will describe each of the funds in detail in Chapter 8, here is a list of the 10 asset classes that make up the Gone Fishin' Portfolio:

1. *U.S. large-cap stocks.* Large-cap is short for large capitalization. (A company's market capitalization is calculated by multiplying the number of shares outstanding by the price per share.) Large-cap stocks are the biggest companies, typically ones with a market capitalization of $5 billion or

more. Historically, they have returned an average of 11% per year. This category includes blue chip household names like Intel, Coca-Cola, IBM, American Express, and General Electric.

2. *U.S. small-cap stocks.* Small-cap stocks are smaller companies, generally with a market capitalization that puts them in the bottom 20%, by size, of the New York Stock Exchange. (These are companies with a market capitalization of $3 billion or less.) Historically, they have returned 12% per year. These returns are slightly better than large-cap stocks, but the price of admission is higher volatility. During rocky periods in the market, small-cap stocks will make you feel like you've entered a bull-riding competition.

3. *European stocks.* Western Europe, of course, has both large and small companies, just like the United States. For the purposes of the Gone Fishin' Portfolio, we'll be using European large-caps.

4. *Pacific Rim stocks.* Here we'll be focusing on large-cap stocks, primarily in Japan, but also in Australia, Hong Kong, Singapore, and New Zealand.

5. *Emerging market stocks.* These are shares of the leading companies in developing markets, primarily in Latin America, Eastern Europe, and Asia.

6. *Precious metals mining stocks.* These are the world's largest gold mining companies. Many of them also produce silver, platinum, and industrial metals.

7. *Real estate investment trusts (REITs).* These are companies that trade like stocks but invest in commercial properties—shopping centers, hotels, apartment complexes, office parks, and warehouses. REITs avoid corporate income taxes by distributing more than 90% of their net cash flow to shareholders each year.

8. *Short-term corporate bonds.* A corporate bond is a company's IOU, a debt security that represents a promise to repay a sum of money at a fixed interest rate over a certain period of time. Short-term bonds generally yield somewhat less than long-term bonds. (Although when the yield curve is inverted, they may yield more.) Their shorter maturities make them less volatile than long-term bonds.

9. *High-yield bonds.* High yield or "junk bonds" are corporate bonds that do not qualify for investment-grade ratings. These bonds pay higher rates of interest because the issuers are less creditworthy. Default rates are higher than on investment-grade bonds as well. (According to Moody's, the annual default rate for BB/Ba bonds is about 1.5%.)

10. *Inflation-adjusted Treasury bonds.* These are U.S. government bonds where the principal moves with inflation, as measured by the Consumer Price Index. The interest rate is fixed, but if there's inflation (and you can pretty much bank on that), you earn that rate on a higher principal value, so your payments actually rise.

As seen in Figure 7.1, *our basic asset allocation is 70% stocks and 30% bonds.* But the suballocation—the types of stocks and bonds we'll use—varies from traditional models. It is designed to be both aggressive enough to boost your long-term returns and uncorrelated enough to smooth out the inevitable bumps along the way.

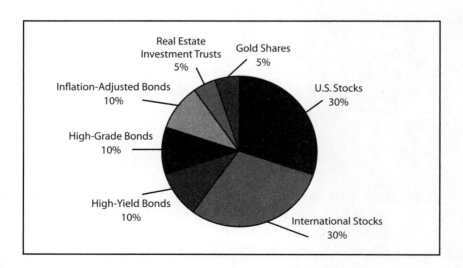

FIGURE 7.1 The Gone Fishin' Asset Allocation

In any given year, these assets will generate returns that may be greater or less than their long-term average. No one can tell you for certain what any of these asset classes will return next year or over the next 10 years. In certain years, the returns for some asset classes will be negative.

Going forward, however, it is reasonable to expect that the long-term returns will be close to their historic averages. Furthermore, by combining these assets we can look forward to earning a handsome return without taking the risk of being fully invested in stocks. That's because these asset classes are not perfectly correlated. In other words, when some zig, others will zag. This reduces the swings in value you'd otherwise see on your statements month to month, and year to year.

For instance, foreign stocks may climb when our domestic market is tanking. U.S. stocks and short-term corporate bonds are actually negatively correlated. That means these bonds are more likely to be rising if U.S. stocks are falling. Gold shares and real estate investment trusts may rally when inflation is higher. And so on.

When you blend your portfolio among assets that give uncorrelated results, you take your first step toward what I call the "Holy Grail of Investing."

Why the Holy Grail? Not because you'll generate eye-popping returns, although that may happen from time to time. The reason I call it the Holy Grail is because investing in the Gone Fishin' Portfolio should generate above-average returns with below-average volatility. And it will allow you to spend your time doing what you want, secure in the knowledge that you are using a system that comes as close to guaranteeing long-term investment success as anything out there.

This is not just my opinion, by the way.

A NOBEL PRIZE-WINNING STRATEGY

In 1990, the Nobel Prize in economics was awarded to Harry Markowitz, Merton Miller, and William Sharpe. They understood that financial markets are extremely efficient at pricing securities.

(That means share prices generally reflect all material, pubic information.) Markowitz's groundbreaking paper "Portfolio Selection," published in *The Journal of Finance,* laid the groundwork for much of today's asset allocation strategies, including the Gone Fishin' Portfolio.

Of course, neither Dr. Markowitz nor anyone else can eliminate uncertainty in the investment process. However, Markowitz won the Nobel Prize for showing how a portfolio constructed of uncorrelated assets can allow you to master uncertainty and generate excellent investment results. He helped define and develop the concept of the efficient frontier, the point where you are generating the best returns within a given level of risk. (It is important to understand that no one can show you the "optimal asset allocation" in advance. This is something that can only be recognized in hindsight.)

Higher returns with less risk. That's the Holy Grail, the goal of the Gone Fishin' Portfolio. Conventional wisdom says it isn't possible. The Nobel Prize committee and decades of experience say it is.

The work done by pioneers such as Gary Brinson, Harry Markowitz, and others provide the philosophical underpinnings of the Gone Fishin' strategy. And there is a mountain of statistical evidence supporting this approach.

In sum, there are two primary reasons you should asset allocate properly. One is to increase returns. The other is to lessen the volatility of a pure stock portfolio. However, I want to remind you that market volatility is not your biggest risk. Inflation is. Volatility can never be eliminated completely without resorting to supersafe investments that leave you vulnerable to this greater risk. Like a slow leak in your pool, inflation gradually drains your purchasing power. You don't feel it in your gut like a bear market in stocks. And you may not notice inflation in the short-term. But it's there year after year, gnawing at your purchasing power like termites in an antebellum mansion.

If you shrink from risk and volatility and keep your money invested in Treasury bills, certificates of deposit, and other cash investments, inflation will win. That creates a diminished standard of living.

Cash investments are fine for setting aside an emergency fund or reaching short-term investment goals. But susceptibility to inflation makes them unsuitable for reaching your long-term investment goals.

THE BEAR MARKET PROTECTION KIT

As we've seen, stocks usually give the best returns when results are measured over decades. Yet from personal experience, I know that many individual investors are unable to patiently ride out the inevitable downturns in the stock market. They become impatient. They become emotional. For this reason, it makes sense to diversify a portion of your investment portfolio into assets that do not move in sync with the broad market. That is why 40% of the Gone Fishin' Portfolio is divided among alternative investments that include REITs, gold shares, and three different types of bond funds. Here's the breakdown:

- REITs—5%
- Gold shares—5%
- Short-term corporate bonds—10%
- High-yield bonds—10%
- Inflation-adjusted Treasuries—10%

Let's look at these asset classes in more detail.

REIT

A REIT is a company that derives its revenue from the management of commercial property. Think of a REIT as a mutual fund made up of hotels, office parks, apartment buildings, shopping centers, or warehouses. Ordinarily, you may find commercial properties like these difficult investments to make, provided your last name isn't Trump or Rockefeller.

But REITs make it possible. These trusts have historically returned 8% a year, a little less than common stocks. But they return more than bonds and don't move in unison with either stocks or bonds. So they reduce the overall volatility of your portfolio.

Bear in mind, there is no guarantee that REITs—or any asset class—will move up when stocks move down. But historically, REITs have often risen—or fallen less—when stocks were going lower.

Gold

We also have a 5% gold allocation. Not to the metal itself, but rather, to shares of precious metals mining companies.

Sure, the physical metal—especially in the form of bullion or numismatic coins—is lovely to behold. But keeping a large quantity of the metal at hand is risky. If you store it safely, there are costs associated with that, too.

More to the point, blue-chip mining shares have returned more than gold over time. And they are a leveraged play on the price of the metal. If gold moves up 10%, gold shares often rally 30% to 40% or more. That's because the gold business is pretty straightforward. You pull the metal out of the ground and sell it at market. There are cash costs for extracting gold and noncash depreciation costs as the value of mines decreases. After overhead and exploration costs, the rest flows to the bottom line. So even a fairly modest increase in the spot price of gold can have a significant impact on earnings.

But here's the number one reason I like gold shares: They are an excellent portfolio diversifier. Gold stocks have just a 0.29 correlation with the S&P 500. That means they generally move independently of the broad market. And that's good news when the broad market is moving south—as it inevitably will from time to time.

Bonds

Lastly, let's look at bonds. When you purchase a bond you are actually lending money to the issuer. When you do, you're promised a return on your investment that is the bond's yield to maturity and the return of the face value of the bond (usually $1,000) at a specified future date, known as the maturity date.

The maturity date may be as far off as 30 years or less than a year. In essence, a bond is simply an IOU, a promissory note that pays interest (usually every six months) until maturity.

Over the long haul, bonds don't generally return as much as stocks, although they have on occasion. (You'd have to go back to 1831 through 1861 to find a 30-year period when the return on either short- or long-term bonds exceeded the return on equities.) The primary benefit of bonds is that they have a low correlation with stocks. So they have a stabilizing effect.

The Gone Fishin' Portfolio employs three types of bonds:

1. *Short-term corporate bonds.* Corporate bonds offer a fixed interest payment over time. That payment does not vary with the profitability of the firm. We will use corporate bonds instead of Treasuries because they pay more. In fact, by owning high-grade, short-term corporate bonds, you can essentially get the same returns as long-term government bonds without the volatility of long-term bonds. As long as we're using bonds to reduce the swings in our portfolio, why not choose the less volatile alternative?

2. *High-yield bonds.* High-yield bonds, also called non–investment-grade bonds, are also corporate bonds. These are bonds rated BBB– or lower by the rating agency Standard & Poor's. They are issued by companies less creditworthy than those that issue investment-grade bonds and are considered speculative. But don't let the name *junk bond* throw you. A diversified portfolio of these bonds, even after accounting for defaults, has returned more than either Treasuries or high-grade corporates. And while they do tend to be more highly correlated with the stock market than other bonds, they do not move in lock step with equities, giving you some diversification advantage.

3. *Inflation-adjusted Treasuries.* Inflation-adjusted Treasuries, more commonly referred to as TIPS (Treasury Inflation-Protected Securities) are the only bonds that guarantee you a return over and above inflation. TIPS pay interest every six months, just like a regular T-bond. But, unlike traditional bonds, your principal increases each year by the amount of inflation, as measured by the consumer price index (CPI). Semi-annual interest payments also increase by the amount of inflation. The interest you receive is exempt from state

and local (but not federal) income taxes. And like other Treasuries, your investment is backed by the full faith and credit of the U.S. government. TIPS are less volatile than traditional bonds. And they are great portfolio diversifiers because they tend to rise when traditional bonds—as well as stocks—are falling.

There has been a long-running debate in the investment community whether it is better to own bonds individually or through a mutual fund. Both ways have their advantages.

If you buy an individual bond, you're guaranteed the return of your principal at maturity. Plus, once you own a bond, there are no ongoing expenses, as there are with bond funds. For these reasons, some investors insist on only owning bonds outright, not through a mutual fund.

But there are disadvantages to owning individual bonds that can make bond mutual funds the better choice. For example, buying (or selling) a bond requires a broker, and that involves commissions. Putting together a diversified bond portfolio requires a much larger investment. You often pay hidden markups and spreads when you trade bonds in the secondary market. And, of course, you cannot automatically reinvest the interest payments. You would have to find a place to put the interest payments to work when you receive them. That entails still more commissions.

If you stick with no-load bond funds, as we will with the Gone Fishin' Portfolio, it's true there are annual expenses you will absorb. But there will be no costs for buying or selling your bonds. You will also enjoy lower minimums, instant diversification, and professional management, and you can arrange to have your fund dividends automatically reinvested.

For most investors, these conveniences make our fixed-income investments both safe and simple. So we'll make good use of bond funds in our Gone Fishin' Portfolio. But we won't overdo it. Stocks are the greatest wealth-creating machine of all time. So our Gone Fishin' Portfolio will have greater exposure to them than bonds.

But we're realistic. We're taking human nature into account, too. It takes nerves of steel—something lacking in most mortals— to place your liquid net worth in a pure stock portfolio and ride out severe bear markets, especially as your portfolio grows in value. For that reason, we'll balance our volatile stock holdings with investments that will act as shock absorbers in the portfolio.

Allocating your assets this way will not only keep your long-term returns high. It should keep your nights restful, too.

REEL IT IN...

1. There are six factors that will determine the long-term value of your investment portfolio: the amount of money you save, the length of time it compounds, your asset allocation, the annual return on those assets, the investment expenses you absorb, and the amount of taxes you pay.
2. Of these six factors, there is only one you can't control: your portfolio's annual return. So we'll concentrate our efforts on the other five.
3. Your asset allocation is your single biggest investment decision. Studies show that over 90% of your portfolio's long-term return is due to this factor alone.
4. Asset allocation is not just diversification. Rather, it means having a strategic mix of noncorrelated assets that will boost returns while lowering risk.
5. The Gone Fishin' Portfolio's basic allocation is 70% stocks and 30% bonds. But its suballocation, which includes REITs, gold shares, and three different types of bonds, is aimed at boosting returns while reducing the volatility of the portfolio as a whole.

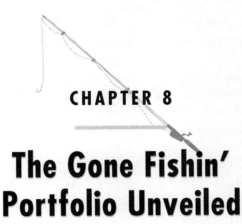

CHAPTER 8

The Gone Fishin' Portfolio Unveiled

"Simplicity is the ultimate sophistication."

—Leonardo da Vinci

You now understand the investment philosophy that underpins the Gone Fishin' Portfolio. In this chapter, I'm going to describe exactly how to put your long-term capital to work—and what you need to do to keep your investments on track year after year. (As I've said from the beginning, the adjustments you need to make to your portfolio will take less than 20 minutes a year.)

Advice this specific is virtually unheard of in the world of investment books. Ordinarily, the author describes general principles and techniques—which may or may not be sound—and then leaves the reader to apply them.

It becomes your responsibility to do the legwork, uncover the right stocks, or analyze the right funds. You're left to survey the investment landscape and make the right decisions. But since there are no specific instructions, most readers probably do little or nothing.

My goal here is different. I'm not going to lay out a smorgasbord of choices. Instead, I've kept it dead simple. I'm going to present a single portfolio designed to meet your long-term investment goals.

Let's get down to brass tacks.

HOW TO PUT YOUR MONEY TO WORK

As I mentioned in Chapter 5, a key component of any long-term portfolio is a healthy exposure to stocks. The asset allocation model I created recommends that you have 30% of your portfolio invested in U.S. stocks and 30% invested in foreign stocks, 5% in REITs, and 5% in gold shares. The remaining 30% we'll divide evenly between three different types of bonds.

As mentioned in Chapter 7, the U.S. stock allocation (30%) should be divided evenly between large-cap and small-cap stocks. Generally speaking, a large-cap stock is one that has a market capitalization of more than $5 billion. (Market capitalization refers to the size of a company, easily calculated by multiplying the number of shares outstanding by the price per share.) Small-cap stocks are those companies with a capitalization of $3 billion or less. (The companies whose size falls between large- and small-cap stocks, as you might expect, are called mid-cap stocks.)

Why are we dividing our money between large and small stocks rather than just buying a single fund? The answer is because these two asset classes behave differently and often give widely varying returns over various periods. From 1982 through 1991, for example, large-cap stocks returned 377%, while small-cap stocks returned only 161%. But from 1995 through 2004, small-cap stocks returned 506%, while large-cap stocks returned only 226%.

Clearly, there are distinct periods—sometimes years, sometimes a decade or more—when one group leads the other. Over long periods, however, small stocks have generally outperformed large ones. True, they're more volatile, but they compensate for it with superior returns.

The international stock allocation (30%) we're going to divide geographically, with one third going into European stocks, one third into Pacific Rim stocks, and one third into emerging market stocks.

Here, specifically, is how to implement the Gone Fishin' strategy using Vanguard mutual funds:

TABLE 8.1 The Gone Fishin' Portfolio

Fund	Symbol	Allocation
Vanguard Total Stock Market Index	VTSMX	15%
Vanguard Small Cap Index	NAESX	15%
Vanguard Emerging Market Index	VEIEX	10%
Vanguard European Index	VEURX	10%
Vanguard Pacific Index	VPACX	10%
Vanguard High Yield Corporate	VWEHX	10%
Vanguard Short Term Investment Grade Bonds	VFSTX	10%
Vanguard Inflation Protected Securities	VIPSX	10%
Vanguard REIT Index	VGSIX	5%
Vanguard Precious Metals and Mining Fund	VGPMX	5%

- *Invest 15% of your portfolio in the Vanguard Total Stock Market Index (VTSMX)*. This fund tracks the broad market, but returns are determined primarily by the performance of U.S. large-cap stocks. Its benchmark is the MSCI U.S. Broad Market Index, a stock index that includes almost all NYSE, Nasdaq, and AMEX stocks. (This index is considerably broader than either the Dow Jones Industrial Average or the S&P 500.) The fund holds a blend of both growth and value stocks. Its expense ratio is 0.15% (compared to 1.12% for the average large-cap stock fund). The fund has returned 10% annually since its inception on April 27, 1992.
- *Invest 15% of your portfolio in the Vanguard Small-Cap Index (NAESX)*. This fund captures the performance of U.S. small-cap stocks. Its benchmark is the MSCI U.S. Small

Cap 1750 Index, a broadly diversified index of smaller U.S. companies. Like the Vanguard Total Stock Market Index, it holds a blend of both growth and value stocks. The annual expense ratio is 0.22% (compared to 1.42% for the average small-cap fund). The fund has returned 11% annually since its inception on October 3, 1960.

Next, we move to international stocks, where you should have 30% of your portfolio invested. Again, we're dividing our investment into separate parts—rather than investing in a single diversified international fund—because the movement of these different assets is often uncorrelated. (This lack of correlation will pay off when we make our annual adjustment to the portfolio, which I'll describe in a moment.)

- *Invest 10% of your portfolio in the Vanguard European Stock Index Fund (VEURX).* This fund's benchmark is the MSCI Europe Index, an index that measures the performance of stocks in more than 15 developed European markets. It holds both growth and value stocks. The annual expense ratio is 0.22% (compared to 1.69% for the average Europe stock fund.) It has returned 10.2% since its inception on June 18, 1990.

- *Invest 10% of your portfolio in the Vanguard Pacific Stock Index Fund (VPACX).* This fund's benchmark is the MSCI Pacific Index, an index that tracks stocks from developed markets in Asia, Australia, and other parts of the Pacific Rim. It, too, holds both growth and value stocks. The annual expense ratio is 0.22% (compared to 1.69% for the average Japan and Asia stock fund). Due to the abysmal performance of the Japanese market since the Nikkei 225 peaked in 1989, the fund has returned only 2.4% a year since inception on June 18, 1990. (Over the long term, these markets are likely to "revert to the mean," giving returns more in line with equity markets elsewhere.)

- *Invest 10% of your portfolio in the Vanguard Emerging Markets Stock Index Fund (VEIEX).* This fund captures the return of major equity markets in Latin America, Eastern Europe, and Southeast Asia. This fund's benchmark is the MSCI Emerging Markets Index. The fund assesses a 0.5% fee ($5 per

$1,000 invested) on purchases. This is not a load. The fee is paid directly to the fund. The fund also assesses a 0.5% fee on redemptions. This fee, too, is paid directly to the fund and is not a load. The annual expense ratio is 0.37% (compared to 1.83% for the average diversified emerging market fund). The fund has returned 10.2% a year since inception on May 4, 1994.

- *Invest 5% of your portfolio in the Vanguard Precious Metals and Mining Fund (VGPMX).* This fund follows the stocks of companies principally involved in mining gold and other metals and minerals. It is not an index fund but is likely to closely track the performance of the S&P/Citigroup Custom Precious Metals and Mining Index. The fund assesses a 1% fee ($10 per $1,000 invested) on sales of shares held for less than one year. (Again, not a load. As a long-term shareholder, you benefit from all the short-term traders who absorb this cost when they cash out of the fund in less than 12 months.) This fund will close to new investors from time to time. (More on that in a moment.) The annual expense ratio is 0.35% (compared to 1.53% for the average precious-metals equity fund). The fund has returned 9.57% a year since inception on May 23, 1984.

- *Invest 5% of your portfolio in the Vanguard REIT Index Fund (VGSIX).* As I described in Chapter 7, these are trusts that allow investors to own an interest in commercial properties, including shopping centers, office parks, hotels, warehouses, industrial centers, and apartment complexes.

    REITs offer several benefits over traditional real estate investments. They are highly liquid, trading on an exchange like a stock. They allow an investor to own a diversified portfolio of properties in a single investment. They also have a fairly low correlation with the stock market, making REITs a great portfolio diversifier.

    The fund's benchmark is the MSCI U.S. REIT Index. The annual expense ratio is 0.21% (compared to 1.47% for the average REIT fund). Here, too, Vanguard assesses a 1% fee on sales of shares held less than one year. The fund has returned 12.9% a year since inception on May 13, 1996.

Now let's move to the fixed-income side, which is the remaining 30% of the portfolio. We know that bonds return less than stocks over time. But they also provide balance and reduce risk in your portfolio. Our asset allocation model suggests that you have 10% of your portfolio in high-grade bonds, 10% in high-yield bonds, and 10% in inflation-adjusted Treasuries.

- *Invest 10% of your portfolio in the Vanguard Short-Term Investment Grade Fund (VFSTX).* The fund's benchmark is the Lehman 1–5 Year U.S. Credit Index. This is an index of corporate and international dollar-denominated bonds with maturities of 1 to 5 years. The annual expense ratio is 0.21% (compared to 96% for the average short-term bond fund). The fund has returned 7.3% per year since its inception on October 29, 1982.
- *Invest 10% of your portfolio in the Vanguard High-Yield Corporate Fund (VWEHX).* This fund's benchmark is the Lehman U.S. High-Yield Index. This index includes mainly intermediate-term corporate bonds with credit ratings at or below Ba1 (Moody's) or BB+ (Standard & Poor's). (Most of the fund's holdings will generally be below investment-grade.) The annual expense ratio is 0.26% (compared to 1.24% for the average high-yield bond fund). The fund assesses a 1% fee on sales of shares held less than a year. This fund has returned 9% a year since inception on December 27, 1978.
- *Invest 10% of your portfolio in the Vanguard Inflation-Protected Securities Fund (VIPSX).* The fund's benchmark is the Lehman U.S. Treasury Inflation Notes Index. The fund's holdings have an average duration of 6.1 years. The expense ratio is 0.2% (compared to 0.92% for the average inflation-protected bond fund). The fund has returned 8.5% a year since inception on June 29, 2000.

Each of these funds has an initial investment minimum of $3,000, and a subsequent investment minimum of $100. Since there are 10 funds that make up the Gone Fishin' Portfolio, this means you will need a minimum of $30,000 to get started. (As I mentioned earlier, if you are a small investor and can't meet this minimum, don't despair. I have a solution for you in Chapter 11 that will allow you to use the same Gone Fishin' strategy using different funds that will allow you to start with smaller amounts.)

Incidentally, you will find more complete information about each of these Vanguard Funds in Appendix A.

YOU MAY QUALIFY FOR EVEN LOWER COSTS

As I've pointed out, Vanguard funds have annual expenses that are the most competitive in the business. In fact, the average mutual fund has expenses that are more than five times those of Vanguard's. This makes a tremendous difference over time. However, you will save even more if you qualify for Vanguard's Admiral Shares.

Admiral Shares are a class of Vanguard funds created to recognize and encourage the cost savings realized from large long-standing accounts. Vanguard passes these savings on to the shareholders who generate them.

There are Admiral Shares available for every fund selection in our Gone Fishin' Portfolio. The ultra-low Admiral Shares expense ratios can reduce your investing expenses anywhere from 18% to 50% below the already low cost of ordinary Vanguard shares.

You are eligible for Admiral Shares if:

- You have $100,000 or more invested in a single Vanguard fund account that offers Admiral Shares. (In fact, Vanguard automatically converts qualifying accounts to Admiral Shares on a quarterly basis.)
- Or, you have owned a single Vanguard fund account for at least 10 years that now has a balance of $50,000 or more, and you're registered for online access to your Vanguard accounts.

Admiral Shares provide you with further significant cost savings. And you will benefit from these savings year after year, because these are not just temporary fee waivers. Admiral shares are a longstanding Vanguard policy. Lower costs means higher net returns to you.

To create your Gone Fishin' Portfolio, you need only visit the Vanguard Web site (www.vanguard.com) or call the company toll-free at 877-662-7447. Vanguard customer service representatives will be happy to answer any questions you have and will send you a prospectus for each of the funds, including the applications. Fill out the applications and return them to Vanguard with your check.

When you've done this—congratulations—you've completed the first step toward handling your serious money in a highly effective way. I'd love to tell you that there's nothing more to do. (Yes, the Gone Fishin' Portfolio is simple. But it's not quite that simple.) There is still one more step you'll need to take, one that will take just a few minutes a year. It's called rebalancing. And it's an important part of our strategy.

HOW TO KEEP YOUR PORTFOLIO ON TRACK

Each fund in the Gone Fishin' Portfolio represents a specific percentage of your total portfolio.

But over time, those percentages will change significantly, depending on the performance of the financial markets. For instance, bonds may finish the year higher, and stocks may be lower. Inflation-adjusted Treasuries may have appreciated, and gold mining shares may have fallen. And so on.

The job of rebalancing is to bring your asset allocation back to our original target percentages. This controls risk. Over the years, it is also likely to deliver a significant performance boost. Why? Because rebalancing requires you to reduce the amount you have invested in the best-performing asset classes and add to those that have underperformed. Since all assets move in cycles, rebalancing forces you to sell high and buy low.

There are essentially two ways to rebalance:

1. You can add new money to those funds that have fallen below your target asset allocation.
2. You can sell a portion of the funds that have risen above your target percentage and add the proceeds to those funds that have fallen below it.

Here's an example. Let's say your initial investment in the Gone Fishin' Portfolio was $100,000. That means you started with the following:

- 15% in U.S. large-cap stocks ($15,000 in the Vanguard Total Stock Market Index)
- 15% in U.S. small-cap stocks ($15,000 in the Vanguard Small-Cap Index)
- 10% in European stocks ($10,000 in the Vanguard European Stock Index Fund)
- 10% in Pacific Rim stocks ($10,000 in the Vanguard Pacific Stock Index Fund)
- 10% in emerging markets ($10,000 in the Vanguard Emerging Markets Index Fund)
- 10% in high-grade bonds ($10,000 in the Vanguard Short-Term Corporate Bond Fund)
- 10% in high-yield bonds ($10,000 in the Vanguard High-Yield Corporate Bond Fund)
- 10% in inflation-adjusted Treasuries ($10,000 in the Vanguard Inflation-Protected Securities Fund)
- 5% in gold shares ($5,000 in the Vanguard Precious Metals and Mining Fund)
- 5% in REITs ($5,000 in the Vanguard Real Estate Investment Trust Index Fund)

At the end of the year, the total value of your portfolio will have changed, and so will the percentage you hold in each fund. Let's say, for example, that your portfolio ends the year worth $122,000.

Your Vanguard Total Stock Market Index may have grown from $15,000 initially to $21,960, for example. That's a nice return. However, U.S. large-cap stocks now represent 18% of your portfolio instead of your target percentage of 15%. And if some assets are now a bigger percentage of your total portfolio, that means other assets are now a smaller percentage.

For example, the real estate fund or the precious metals equity fund may represent less than 5% each of your total portfolio value. If you have enough cash to make up the difference, you can simply add money to each fund that has lagged until it reaches our original target percentage.

This way is preferable because it means you're not creating a taxable event by selling something. (Taking profits involves paying capital gains taxes, unless you hold this portfolio in a retirement account.) It's also positive because, as I mentioned in the chapter on saving, it really pays to keep adding to your investments over time. It is one of the few steps you can take that is guaranteed to help you reach your financial goals more quickly.

However, using the previous example, if you didn't have the cash to invest, you would need to redeem $3,660 worth of the Vanguard Total Stock Market Fund and put the proceeds into those funds that have fallen below your target percentages. (You would do this by simply calling Vanguard's toll-free number and asking the representative to make the changes for you.)

To rebalance your portfolio each year without adding money to your account, you simply redeem part of those funds that have risen above your target percentages and add the proceeds to those that have declined below your target percentages. It's as simple as that.

The Beauty of Rebalancing

When should you do this? You should do it approximately once a year. The exact date you do it is not important. But there needs to be an interval of at least a year and a day between each time you set your portfolio and rebalance.

Why? Number one, you'll avoid paying short-term capital gains taxes by waiting at least a year and a day. (The long-term capital gains rate is a maximum of 15%. Short-term capital gains taxes, by contrast, can be as high as 35%.) Second, you'll avoid paying the 1% redemption fee on investments held less than a year in the Vanguard High-Yield Bond Fund, Vanguard Real Estate Investment Trust Index Fund, and Vanguard Emerging Markets Stock Index Fund.

Again, unless your investments are held entirely in a qualified retirement plan—like an IRA or 401(k)—where a fund redemption is not a taxable event, *it's preferable to rebalance your portfolio by adding money to those funds that have fallen below your original target percentages.*

Of course, as your portfolio grows in value it becomes increasingly unlikely that you will save enough each year to avoid selling something during the rebalancing process. (Unless, of course, your income and/or savings rate grows dramatically.)

Adding to those sectors that are down sounds simple enough. But I can tell you from working with hundreds of investors that most have a strong compulsion to add to those assets that are performing best, not those that are performing worst. Long-term investors need to fight this instinct and think like Ebenezer Scrooge instead. Forget what the hot asset class is doing. You want to buy what's cheapest for the long-term advantage it confers.

As investment great John Templeton has said, "To buy when others are despondently selling and to sell when others are avidly buying requires the greatest fortitude and pays the greatest reward."

Don't thwart the power of this strategy by succumbing to the temptation to buy more of your winning funds. Given enough time, each asset class will experience a down cycle. That's when you'll add to them. When they're cheap and out of favor. Not when they're popular and expensive.

The beauty of our rebalancing strategy is that it provides you with a clear discipline of what to sell and when. Remember, it's impossible to predict which asset class will be the best- or worst-performing in any given year. So although international stocks, for example, may have underperformed last year, there is no way of being certain that they won't be one of the top performers this year or next. And even if an asset class experiences several years in a row of lackluster performance, which is not uncommon, it's important that you not stray from your discipline.

Regardless of what happens from one year to the next, the advantages of rebalancing are much clearer over a decade or more. By adding to your lagging assets, you may occasionally feel like you're throwing good money after bad. You're not.

Research from Ibbotson Associates conclusively demonstrates that the strategy of rebalancing reduces the level of portfolio risk in both market upturns and downturns. But it found that the risk reduction is greater during market downturns.

It's not hard to understand why. Stocks give the best returns over time. But when the stock market is performing poorly, a rebalanced portfolio is less likely to experience negative returns than one that isn't rebalanced.

There is a lot of debate among asset allocators about how frequently you should rebalance. Some say once a year, some say every 18 months, still others argue some other time period works best.

The important thing is that you do rebalance. Buying funds and just holding them through thick and thin isn't the wisest course. Since stocks appreciate the most over time, they will eventually make up the overwhelming majority of your portfolio. Without rebalancing, the older you get, the more volatile your portfolio will become. That's probably not what you want.

In short, the Gone Fishin' Portfolio requires you to take only one action a year, rebalancing. It not only reduces volatility, it is essential to maximizing your returns. (Studies show that annual rebalancing can enhance portfolio returns about 1% a year.) It also helps instill the discipline required for investment success.

So do it. And keep doing it, year after year.

PUTTING THE GONE FISHIN' PORTFOLIO TO THE TEST

The Gone Fishin' Portfolio—rebalanced annually—has compounded at 17.3% annually in the five years since I created it in 2003. That's considerably better than the return of the S&P 500 over the same period. And it was less risky than being fully invested in stocks. (After all, 30% of our portfolio is in bonds.)

Of course, a lot of investment strategies work in a rising market. Yet they often lag when the market takes a tumble. However, the Gone Fishin' Portfolio would have beaten the S&P 500 every year in the last bear market, too.

If you had owned it in the bear market of 2000 to 2002, for example, you would have seen it decline 6.1% in 2000, 2.7% in 2001, and 5.4% in 2002.

These are temporary declines that most investors can live with. The S&P 500, by contrast, fell harder: down 10.1% in 2000, down 13% in 2001, and down 23.4% in 2002. (See Figure 8.1 and Table 8.2.)

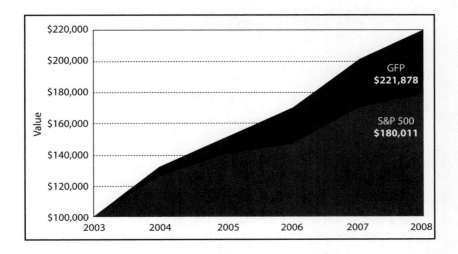

FIGURE 8.1 Gone Fishin' Portfolio vs. S&P 500 from 2003 to 2007

Don't get me wrong. I cannot guarantee that the Gone Fishin' Portfolio will beat the S&P every year. Of course, no other strategy can, either. But, for reasons explained in a moment, there is good cause to believe it will continue to outperform in the years ahead.

First, let's look back a little further and see how you would have done had you held the Gone Fishin' Portfolio, and rebalanced annually, over the last decade.

As the stock market climbed in the late 1990s, you would have steadily reduced your exposure to fast-appreciating equities and added to lagging areas like bonds, REITs, and mining shares.

TABLE 8.2 Gone Fishin' Portfolio Annual Return vs. S&P 500 Annual Return for Each Individual Year from 2000 to 2007

Year	GFP	S&P 500
2000	−6.14%	−9.11%
2001	−2.73%	−11.89%
2002	−5.41%	−22.10%
2003	32.72%	28.68%
2004	15.28%	10.88%
2005	11.93%	4.91%
2006	16.99%	15.80%
2007	10.75%	5.49%

At the time, this felt to most investors like exactly the wrong thing to do. After all, stocks were on fire, and these other assets were going nowhere or, worse, down. But history teaches us that all markets move in cycles. And when stocks got pummeled, what ended up soaring in value? Sure enough, it was the alternative assets like bonds, REITs, and gold shares.

Following the Gone Fishin' strategy of asset allocating and rebalancing would have allowed you to trim your generous profits during the bull market of the 1990s. It would also have saved your hide and protected most of your gains during the bear market of the next three years.

Of course, more good things would have happened if you had stuck to this discipline. As stocks hit new lows in 2000, 2001, and 2002, you would have kept rebalancing your portfolio. What then? A whole new bull market started and all those stocks that you bought when they were cheap were now rocketing higher once more. Before long, in fact, the market was hitting new all-time highs.

By now you know the drill. That means when it came time to rebalance, you were once again selling the asset classes that had appreciated the most and adding to those that were cheapest.

As I said before, this system doesn't just aim for you to buy low and sell high. It forces you to. And that gives you a significant performance boost.

A SIMPLE STRATEGY IN A COMPLEX WORLD

I don't pretend that the Gone Fishin' Portfolio is the only way to manage your long-term money effectively. I only claim that it works. I don't know an alternative strategy that has a greater probability of success—or requires less time.

Incidentally, there is a limit to how far back you can test the Gone Fishin' Portfolio—and for a simple reason. This strategy requires you to invest 10% in inflation-adjusted Treasuries. However, Uncle Sam only created these securities in 1997. (Also, the Vanguard Inflation-Protected Securities Fund wasn't launched until June 29, 2000. In the hypothetical example above, I substituted the performance of TIPS themselves for the three years prior to the Vanguard fund's debut.)

Of course, you cannot know for certain what this portfolio (or any other) will return in the future, no matter how much back-testing you do. As I've said from the beginning, to a large extent uncertainty will always be your companion. Historical asset class returns are a valuable guidepost. They are not a guarantee.

However, it's not just the attractiveness of past or future returns that make the Gone Fishin' Portfolio such a compelling choice. It's also the fact that it requires so little attention.

I have a tennis pal, for instance, who spends hours each day trading S&P 500 futures. Is he making money? He says he is. But is he really making enough to justify the hundreds of hours he spends doing it each year? I wonder. (And I notice he hasn't given up his day job.)

The Gone Fishin' Portfolio is designed for those who want a powerful and sophisticated system for managing their money, but who prefer to dedicate their time and energy to the things they value most, whether that's growing prize tomatoes, playing Pebble Beach, or reeling in marlin off Costa Rica's Pacific coast.

If this strategy is so great, you may wonder why your investment advisor hasn't recommended it. I tried to make that clear in the early chapters. The Gone Fishin' Portfolio spells doom for them. It generates no brokerage commissions, no planning fees, no sales loads, and no wrap fees.

It's true we all need to rely on banks and insurance companies for some financial services. But do you need to use them—or anyone else—to manage your money, too?

Absolutely not. Armed with the investment basics and a little discipline, you can manage your serious money yourself—and save many thousands of dollars in the process. The folks on the other side of the desk may argue that the world of investing is so complicated—and your financial circumstances so unique—that it's foolhardy for you to consider managing your money yourself.

Investing can, of course, be a complicated subject. But you also have the choice of keeping it simple. That's what the Gone Fishin' Portfolio does. It keeps effective, sophisticated money management simple.

If you like engaging in short-term stock trading as a hobby, by all means, continue to enjoy it. I do it myself. This is something you don't generally hear from hard-core asset allocators, incidentally.

But let's face it. You can invest your long-term growth money safely and have some fun in the market, too. The two activities are not mutually exclusive.

It is important, however, to segregate your long-term core portfolio (like the Gone Fishin' Portfolio) from your short-term trading portfolio. This keeps things uncomplicated. Plus, it ensures that you don't start trading your long-term positions or find yourself clinging to your short-term trades.

In my view, even the most dedicated short-term traders need an effective long-term strategy like Gone Fishin' for their serious money. And if you would rather spend eight hours in 10-degree weather shoveling snow than analyze mountains of financial data, well, the Gone Fishin' Portfolio may be all you need.

My hunch is that the vast majority of folks have better things to do with their time than watch the "ticker tape." It's for them that I've written this book. And for those, too, who want some insurance to back up their trading activities.

In short, with the Gone Fishin' Portfolio you can manage your money yourself. You can do it with just as much sophistication as the country's leading money mangers—and get better results than the vast majority of them. You can do an end run around Wall Street's marketing machine that wants to "capture your assets" and live off your investments. *Best of all, the whole program requires a commitment of less than 20 minutes a year.*

I don't think that's too much to ask when the goal is financial freedom.

Incidentally you can track the progress of this portfolio—and keep abreast of any new developments—at gonefishinportfolio.com.

Managing your money this way is likely to lead to superior long-term investment returns. Moreover, this strategy is designed to make sure you never lose. After all, you have removed three layers of risk—active manager risk, individual security risk, and high expenses—that could potentially derail your retirement plans or cause you to fail to meet your investment objectives.

Our goal here is not to beat the market by the largest margin in the shortest period of time. Rather, it's to allow you to achieve financial independence and its most important by-product: peace of mind.

WHAT TO TELL THE NAYSAYERS

There are some aspects of the Gone Fishin' strategy that critics— and fee-oriented investment advisors—may find controversial. I want to address those potential objections now. Some, for example, may object to the inclusion of asset classes like gold shares and junk bonds. Others will question the weightings of different asset classes. Still others will question the "one-size-fits-all" nature of this strategy. I'm happy to rebut them all.

Unusual Success from Unusual Assets

Let's begin by looking at the reasons for the inclusion of more controversial asset classes like gold shares, foreign stocks (particularly emerging market stocks), and high-yield bonds. In my view, the key to diversifying wisely is including investments that tend to be out of sync with the rest of your holdings.

I've mentioned that the Gone Fishin' Portfolio has returned 17.3% annually in the five years since its inception. The vast majority of asset allocation models have not performed this well over the same period. A big reason for the outperformance of this portfolio is its somewhat unconventional makeup. Many asset allocation models have nothing more than a U.S. stock fund, a U.S. bond fund, and cash.

That plain vanilla approach is unlikely to do as well in the future as our Gone Fishin' strategy. It doesn't allow you to benefit from investment opportunities overseas, the inflation protection available from TIPS, and other alternative investments like junk bonds, gold shares, and REITs.

Holding a lot of cash is like dragging an anchor. If it makes you feel comfortable, keep enough money in cash in the bank to cover a year's worth of living expenses. But don't include it in your long-term portfolio. Cash does nothing to boost your long-term returns.

Excluding these lesser-owned assets is a shortcoming of other investment models. The performance of the Gone Fishin' Portfolio testifies to that. But let's examine the rationale, starting with high-yield bonds.

A 10% exposure to the high-yield bond market is one of the reasons the Gone Fishin' Portfolio has beaten the S&P 500, while taking less risk than being fully invested in stocks. Despite the pejorative name "junk," these bonds offer a number of advantages.

Number one, high-yield bonds have traditionally returned more than investment-grade bonds. For example, the Vanguard High-Yield Corporate Fund, which has been around for almost 30 years, has returned 9% annually since its inception. The Vanguard Total Bond Market Index Fund has returned only 6.7% in the more than two decades it has been around. What's not to like about the high-yield numbers?

Second, high-yield bonds have a fairly low correlation with investment-grade bonds, like Treasuries and AAA corporates. That's what we want when we asset allocate. Third, owning a professionally managed, broadly diversified portfolio of high-yield bonds is a lot less risky than owning just a handful of individual bonds.

Blending high-yield bonds with the other nine asset categories actually reduces your overall portfolio volatility while increasing your returns.

Still, many asset allocators give them a pass. Here are the three leading objections, along with my response:

1. *You invest in bonds for safety.* That's true, but putting riskier assets in your portfolio increases the return of the portfolio as a whole. (And, technically, junk bonds are safer than stocks because they represent a senior claim on the assets of the company.)

2. *High-yield bonds are extremely tax-inefficient.* Yes, their interest payments are taxed at your marginal tax rate, not the lower capital gains rate. But you can avoid this problem by owning them in your IRA or other qualified retirement plan, as I describe more fully in Chapter 10.

3. *High-yield bonds are more closely correlated to stocks than investment grade bonds.* True again. But so what? The two asset classes don't move in lock step and there are plenty of periods when high-yield bonds perform better than equities.

To those who insist high-yield bonds are simply too risky to include, remember the words of junk bond king Michael Milken: The rating on triple-A bonds only has one way to go—down. Sure, most investment-grade obligations maintain their standing. But in no case do triple-A-bonds receive upgrades.

In short, including a 10% allocation to high-yield bonds gives you an edge. Historically, portfolios that include exposure to this asset class have performed better than those that rely solely on investment-grade bonds for the fixed-income allocation.

Incidentally, some investors may ask why our high-grade bond component consists of short-term investment-grade bonds, rather than long-term Treasuries.

The first reason is that the historical return has only been about 1.5% less per year than long-term bonds, despite a much lower level of volatility. Another is that there is a small but fairly consistent negative correlation between short-term bonds and stocks. If we own these bonds not to boost our returns but rather to get us through the inevitable sinking spells in the market without abandoning our discipline, then short-term bonds are the superior choice.

Another Glittering Asset

Next let's turn to our inclusion of gold shares. This may seem questionable to some. After all, despite the sharp run-up in gold prices over the past few years, it wasn't until 2007 that gold finally surpassed the $800 mark it hit back in 1980.

As I mentioned in the section on long-term asset returns, gold has generally been dead weight in a long-term portfolio, despite flashes of brilliance from time to time.

Throughout the book, I've referred to more than 200 years of stock market returns. We have much more data on the historical price of gold. A few millennia-worth, in fact. And, in inflation-adjusted terms, the long-term return on the so-called barbarous relic is essentially *zero*. That's right, gold has worked well as a store of value, but as an investment it has been the pits. (This isn't too surprisingly when you consider that for centuries gold *was* money.)

However, gold shares—and other precious metals equities—are another story. They have performed quite well. In fact, while gold shares have been traded on the major U.S. and foreign exchanges for hundreds of years, until recently there has been no reliable precious metals equity index. This, in itself, is the reason many traditional asset allocators have excluded them from their portfolios. But I believe that's a mistake.

On his Web site efficientfrontier.com, William Bernstein has written a brief paper called "The Expected Return of Precious Metals Equity." In it, he says:

> One can cobble together a "precious metals index" which will estimate the long-term return of this asset. The Morningstar database of mutual funds has a precious metals fund index which goes back to 1976, and before that the Van Eck International Fund, which started operations in 1956, became a precious metals fund sometime in 1968. Combining the Van Eck data for 1969–75 with the Morningstar data beginning in 1976 provides a 27.75 year time series—just long enough to provide a reasonable estimate of the "true" long-term return of this asset. The results are startling—the annualized return from January 1969 to September 1996 was 12.81 percent. This is actually *higher* than the S&P 500 (11.24%), U.S. small-cap stocks (12.44%), and the EAFE (12.52%) for the same period.

The returns have been even better since then due to the strong performance of gold itself. However, the long-term returns data for both REITs and gold shares are somewhat suspect. But they are each good inflation hedges. And while gold bullion has generated a dismal long-term return, gold shares have a history of doing well. Better still, they tend to move independently of the stock and bond markets. Gold-related investments have a near zero correlation with other asset classes. That makes them great portfolio diversifiers. That's especially true when you rebalance. Including a gold fund as a small component of a diversified portfolio helps you balance your overall portfolio risk. That's why I recommend a 5% gold share allocation.

However, the Vanguard Gold and Precious Metals Fund closed "temporarily" in February, 2006. There are two primary reasons. One is that the fund was experiencing a high influx of fresh money, yet the universe of gold stocks is quite small. The total market capitalization of the world's top 15 gold companies is approximately $100 billion. (That's about a fifth of the market cap of ExxonMobil.) A whole lot of money chasing a small set of stocks—as we learned during the Internet bubble at the turn of the millennium—distorts prices. That makes it tough for the manager to put the money to work prudently. Plus, if accepted, these inflows would increase the fund's trading costs. So, as I write, the Vanguard Gold and Precious Metals Fund is closed to new investors, with two exceptions.

If you are a current holder of this fund, Vanguard will allow you to add to your holdings. Or if you are a Vanguard Flagship client—with total assets at the fund company totaling more than $1,000,000—you can still buy the fund.

If you are not a current holder of this fund and don't meet Vanguard's hefty Flagship minimum, you will need to substitute either another no-load gold mutual fund or an exchange-traded gold share index like Market Vectors Gold Miners (AMEX: GDX). (More on this in Chapter 11.)

The World Is Your Oyster

Lastly, some advisors may take issue with our heavy exposure to international equity markets. We're audacious, some say, to put half our equity money in foreign shares. But U.S. stocks account for only about 40% of the world's market capitalization. The rest of the world accounts for 60%. It makes sense to build an equity portfolio that reflects the success of capitalism in our increasingly borderless world.

According to Global Insight, a comprehensive provider of economic, financial, and political analysis, in the early 1980s, the United States accounted for a third of the global economy. In the next 20 years, that share could be cut in half. It's reasonable to expect that growth of this magnitude will positively influence foreign share prices.

However, I'll concede this is an area where Vanguard founder Jack Bogle and I disagree. For example, he writes in *Common Sense on Mutual Funds* that "Overseas investments—holdings in the corporations of other nations—are not essential, nor even necessary, to a well-diversified portfolio."

Bogle and some others believe that the big U.S. multinational firms that make up a substantial percentage of U.S. stock indexes give you all the international exposure you need. As for diversification value, they argue that world markets fell in concert during the stock market crash of 1987 and the brief crisis of 1998 (when hedge fund Long Term Capital fell apart). My response is, yes, we've seen short-term panics that caused investors worldwide to rush to the sidelines in unison. But after brief periods when global markets moved in concert, individual country markets reverted to fluctuations based on events in their local markets.

An excellent case for diversifying outside your home country— whatever it may be—is Japan, the world's second largest stock market. In the 1980s, the return on Japan's Nikkei 225 index dominated all other world markets, returning 28.4 percent per year. The U.S. market returned 17.4% per year during the same period, and other non–U.S. markets only 16.5%.

But Japan's fortunes reversed in the 1990s. Japan's economy stumbled and the market declined 1% per year for the decade. Contrast that with 13.5% annual returns for non-Japan international markets and 18.2% per year in the United States over the period.

An American investor would have benefited from exposure to Japan in the 1980s. And clearly the Japanese equity investor would have been wise to spread investment risk beyond Japan's borders in the 1990s. Few—if any—investors were able to predict Tokyo's dramatic advance or the grinding decline. But it didn't matter, so long as you asset allocated properly, rebalanced regularly, and stuck with the program. The key is to invest a set percentage in foreign equity markets and stay with them through thick and thin.

If you don't diversify into foreign markets, you suffer an opportunity cost, the loss of currency diversification, and a potential rebalancing advantage.

Moreover, it's important to realize that the world is becoming increasingly integrated economically. Trade is increasing worldwide. Taxes and tariffs are coming down. Accounting standards are becoming more transparent.

Yes, the United States is still the world's leading economic power and likely to remain so for many years to come. But why be provincial? Americans are already patronizing hundreds of international companies, such as Royal Dutch, Samsung, Sony, Nestle, and Honda, whether they recognize it or not. Why would you be willing to buy these companies' products but not the companies themselves?

For example, when you get up in the morning, you may turn on your Japanese TV to check the news, have a cup of Brazilian coffee, put on your shirt made in Taiwan, your shoes from Italy, and your Swiss watch, before getting in your German car for the commute to work.

Earnings growth, too, is often stronger in overseas markets. Stock valuations are often better. And currency fluctuations provide you with further diversification for your portfolio.

Of course, if putting half of your money in international markets is considered heresy, some investors will really flip their wigs about putting roughly 17% of your equity money—10% of your total portfolio—in emerging markets.

"If I wouldn't vacation in these places," a client once told me, "why should I send my investment capital there?" Higher potential returns and a portfolio that exhibits less overall volatility are two good reasons. So far, this strategy has paid off handsomely in the Gone Fishin' Portfolio. I believe it will in the decades ahead, too.

Sure, the stock markets of Latin America, Eastern Europe, and Southeast Asia can get pretty bumpy occasionally. They tend to have more frequent political and economic problems. Their currencies are less secure. Their markets are often less regulated. But there are advantages, too.

Remember, 50 years ago, Germany and Japan were emerging markets. Fifty years before that, the United States was an emerging market. And two centuries ago, England, France, and Holland were, too. Betting on these countries when they were emerging markets paid off pretty darn well.

Still, some will ask, "But why take the risk?" As I've said before, people today are living longer than ever. If you don't want your money to give out before your pulse does, you need your portfolio to do some heavy lifting. In the decades ahead, as emerging markets gradually turn into developed markets, they may well be the afterburners in your portfolio.

In short, holding riskier assets—like emerging markets, gold stocks, and high-yield bonds —should give your portfolio a boost it wouldn't get holding tamer assets. And the fact that these assets are relatively uncorrelated should cause your total portfolio to experience less overall volatility, not more.

True, our particular asset allocation is a bit unconventional. That means it will have years—or a string of them—when the returns may be radically different from those of the S&P 500. But over the long haul, if you've kept saving and rebalancing, your total return should be ample to meet your retirement needs.

THERE IS ONLY ONE OBJECTIVE

Lastly, I expect to catch some flak for recommending a single long-term portfolio, rather than suggesting you customize your asset allocation based on your personal circumstances.

This is not the heresy some might imagine, however. The Gone Fishin' Portfolio is designed for long-term capital appreciation. It is not the way to save for a down payment on a house. It is not the way to invest your 15-year-old daughter's college money. It's not the way for a retiree to maximize monthly investment income.

It is a growth portfolio designed to keep you from outliving your money. It should give satisfactory returns for 25-year-olds just beginning to invest, as well as 65-year-olds whose retirement may realistically last three decades, before they go to that big retirement home in the sky.

I'll be the first to concede that once you reach the late stage of life where your primary (or sole) objective is to structure your portfolio for maximum income and capital preservation, you need to make your asset allocation more conservative.

Still, the question remains: Does someone who realistically has a decade or more of life ahead of him truly need someone to assess his "personal risk tolerance" and design a customized asset allocation?

My answer is no. As the pioneering fund manager John Templeton once said, "For all long-term investors, there is only one objective—maximum total return after taxes."

Yet some investment advisors seem to be planning for another objective: their clients' inability to stick with the program, even if that means they won't meet their long-term investment objectives. We all know that when the market begins acting badly, as it will from time to time, it can be stressful. However, if your choice is between a few restless nights and a comfortable retirement or sleeping like a baby and waking up one day to find you're out of money and too old to go back to work, what is your best choice? Unless you've accumulated enough to coast into retirement, you can't have it both ways.

A typical question that fund companies and financial planners ask is, "During market declines, would you sell portions of your riskier assets and invest the money in safer assets?" Of course, millions of investors have done exactly this during market declines over the years. And almost as many millions have regretted it later.

For an investor to sell into a short-term market decline goes against everything the past has to teach us. We have more than 200 years of stock market history—valuable hindsight—demonstrating that every decline was a buying opportunity for the long-term investor, even the Great Depression.

Instead of setting up a conservative asset allocation based on the likelihood that you'll panic and sell during the next correction or bear market, why not simply resolve that you won't do it. And if you can't resist feeling panicky, at least keep yourself from selling. Instead of structuring your portfolio for future ineptitude, educate yourself now so you're able to show some backbone when the chips are down.

Another typical question from those who insist on assessing an investor's personal investment style is, "Would you invest in a mutual fund based solely on a brief conversation with a friend, coworker, or relative?"

If you answer yes to this question, I applaud your honesty. But that's all I applaud. Again, the only purpose this question serves is to verify whether the advisor is dealing with someone who is unsophisticated. Unsophisticated investors, however, generally have the same long-term financial requirements as sophisticated ones—namely, a comfortable retirement.

If you buy hot tips, try to time the market, or take unsolicited advice from co-workers, your "golden" years are likely to look more like scrap metal. Is it possible that unsophisticated investors can meet their financial goals by taking less risk than sophisticated investors? I don't think so. The right portfolio is the right portfolio. Don't create a conservative portfolio that virtually guarantees you less money in retirement. Structure your investments for the best prospective returns and stick with your plan. That's what successful investing is about.

I'm not being flip here. I realize that volatile markets create a lot of anxiety, especially when we're talking about the money that will fund your lifestyle in retirement.

But let's face facts. We can't eliminate volatility. We can't eliminate uncertainty. And we can't eliminate the fearful emotions that we experience when the market swoons from time to time, as it will. I can only alert you to how you're likely to feel and suggest how you can keep these emotions from undoing the good work you've done. (In fact, I've dedicated much of Chapter 13 to this topic.)

So why do so many financial planners insist that they need to "personalize" your long-term investment portfolio? One reason is it helps justify their fees. Another reason is it reduces their legal liabilities. Brokers and other investment advisors are supposed to "know their customers." They have a multitude of onerous regulatory requirements, some of them largely meaningless.

Listen to Jim Otar, for example, a certified financial planner, independent advisor and the author of *High Expectations and False Dreams: One Hundred Years of Stock Market History Applied to Retirement Planning.*

He has spent a lot of time researching and writing about the perfect portfolio for retirement. In June 2002, he wrote a column on "Client Strategies" in the journal *Financial Planning* for fellow CFPs. He writes that, with very few exceptions, "The optimum asset allocation for an income portfolio has nothing to do with your client's risk tolerance, his investment knowledge or many other countless questions that your clients are forced to answer during your initial interview. Other than fulfilling the regulatory requirements, the ritual of risk assessment has no significance to the optimum asset mix."

Some advisors will argue that their clients can't withstand the volatility inherent in stocks. Fine. But are they also telling them that they aren't likely to meet their long-term investment goals as a result? Wouldn't it be better to educate them and reassure them rather than just throw in the towel with a portfolio that is too conservative from the start? Because unless you're worth so much that you have the luxury of investing purely for income and preservation of capital, you need a healthy exposure to stocks.

Rest assured, you'll still experience volatility with the Gone Fishin' Portfolio because you'll own some higher risk assets. But as William Bernstein writes in *The Intelligent Asset Allocator*, "Appreciate that diversified portfolios behave very differently than the individual assets in them, in much the same way that a cake tastes different from shortening, flour, butter and sugar."

In other words, your whole portfolio will fluctuate less than some of its constituent parts. And, if the next 30 years are anything like the last 30, you'll outperform the vast majority of professional money managers. Best of all, you'll be headed down the path to financial independence. And you'll have the satisfaction and cost-savings of doing it on your own.

Of course, it's reasonable to ask how you can be sure the asset allocation I've recommended here is the very best one for the future. The truth is you can't. Like so many other factors we've discussed, you simply cannot know in advance the "very best" asset allocation. The "perfect" asset allocation is something that can only be recognized in hindsight.

The most important thing is to avoid a poor asset allocation. What would that be? Easily, one of the worst is 100% cash. An allocation that is light on equities generally won't work. And an asset allocation that changes like the seasons is unlikely to get the job done either.

The Gone Fishin' Portfolio offers you excellent prospects. It divides your investment capital among a number of high-returning but uncorrelated assets. It contains some more unconventional asset classes that should give you a performance boost over time. And the portfolio has a proven track record, beating the S&P 500 every year since its inception with less risk than being fully invested in stocks.

Still, you might ask, isn't recommending a single asset allocation needlessly prescriptive? Perhaps. But there's another reason I've recommended a specific portfolio.

In my experience, the more choices an investor has, the less likely he or she is to get off the dime and actually put their money to work. By making things dead simple, I'm trying to give you that final nudge. In essence, I'm telling you there's nothing left to figure out. Here's the portfolio. Go do it.

UNDERSTAND THE GAME TO WIN IT

George Bernard Shaw once said, "Liberty requires responsibility. That is why most men dread it."

The Gone Fishin' Portfolio is designed for responsible adults. Financial freedom requires that you not only plan to do the right thing, but actually do it. This is true of every successful investment strategy. I'm just being blunt.

Don't make your portfolio too conservative now to prepare for emotionally overwrought behavior later. Plan for success, instead. Realize that a smiling broker or financial planner will be happy to move your money in and out of the market and hold your hand year after year. (Just bear in mind that this handholding is not for love. It comes at a hefty price.)

I've sometimes reminded my readers that stock market investing is a lot like football. If you're going to play the game, you're going to get knocked down from time to time. If your son or grandson came to you and told you that he wanted to be a Heismann trophy winner, that he dreams of nothing but running and scoring, you might remind him that he's also going to have a lot of sore Mondays, too. To believe otherwise wouldn't be realistic. Getting the stuffing knocked out of you is part of the game.

The same is true with investing. If you're going after the kind of returns that only volatile assets can provide, don't be surprised when the volatility shows up. Our asset allocation will provide the pads and helmet. But you're still going to get hit from time to time. Don't let that deter you. Your long-term returns should be more than satisfactory. That's what leads to investment success . . . and a comfortable retirement.

REEL IT IN...

1. To put your money to work in the Gone Fishin' Portfolio, invest your money as I describe in Table 8.1.
2. Rebalance your portfolio once a year to increase returns and control risk. You can do this by adding new money to lagging assets or by selling a portion of your best-performing assets and applying the proceeds toward those that have lagged, or both.
3. By rebalancing annually, you will force yourself to buy low and sell high—the essence of successful investing.
4. The make-up of the Gone Fishin' Portfolio is unconventional. But riskier assets like gold shares, emerging-market stocks, and high-yield bonds are included to keep future returns higher and portfolio risk lower than would be possible using a more conventional asset allocation.
5. The Gone Fishin' Portfolio is designed to reduce volatility, but it cannot eliminate it. That means you need to have realistic expectations. It's okay to have down quarters—and even down years—in the pursuit of high long-term returns.

CHAPTER 9

Why the Gone Fishin' Portfolio Is Your Best Investment Plan

"He who wishes to be rich in a day will be hanged in a year."

—Leonardo da Vinci

The Gone Fishin' Portfolio is an investment system that will save you time, money, and endless headaches. It's simple, yes. But don't be fooled by its simplicity.

The Yale Endowment and the California Public Employees' Retirement System, the nation's largest pension fund, are using similar systems. Run your money this way and you can count yourself among the nation's most sophisticated investors.

The Gone Fishin' Portfolio will allow you to generate above-average returns with below-average risk for decades to come.

When you put this system to work, you will be light years ahead of the typical investor who is either wondering what the heck to do, learning the hard way, or turning things over to an investment professional who, if any good, will do something similar at a much higher cost, or, if not so good, will deliver subpar returns, along with high fees, for as long as he allows it.

So, congratulate yourself. You are joining an elite minority who are securing their financial future by managing risk intelligently.

THE PLAN THAT OUTPERFORMS PROFESSIONAL MONEY MANAGERS

Before we discuss why the Gone Fishin' Portfolio is your best investment choice, let's take a moment to review:

1. Everyone should have a workable, battle-tested investment philosophy as the foundation of his investment strategy.
2. Acknowledge that the future is always uncertain. No one can consistently forecast interest rates, inflation, the economy, or the performance of the financial markets.
3. Investment success begins with meaningful saving. You need to save as much as you can, for as long as you can, beginning as soon as you can.
4. No one cares more about the net return on your portfolio than you. You should manage your money yourself.
5. Most Americans are living longer, healthier lives. Many baby boomers retiring at age 65 will spend up to three decades in retirement. That means unless you're independently wealthy, you need to skip the ultraconservative choices and seek maximum total returns, so your money lasts as long as you do.
6. There are six factors that will determine the long-term value of your portfolio: the amount you save, the length of time you let it compound, your asset allocation, your portfolio's annual returns, your investment expenses, and taxes.
7. Your asset allocation is your most important investment decision. Although no one can tell you the single best asset

allocation in advance, you need one that offers an excellent chance of long-term success.

8. No-load index funds with low annual expenses and high tax efficiency are the best vehicle for implementing your investment strategy.

9. You need to rebalance approximately once a year to boost returns and reduce risk.

10. In the end, the best investors are not necessarily smarter, just more disciplined.

By sticking to the Gone Fishin' strategy—by saving, asset allocating, rebalancing, and keeping an eye on taxes and expenses—you can look forward both to reaching your long-term investment goals and outperforming the vast majority of professional money managers.

This last claim—beating the professional managers—is likely to be a sticking point with some investors. Many of them will accept the evidence that their asset allocation is the primary driver of their portfolios' total returns. But wouldn't the returns be better if we searched for the best managers in each asset class instead of settling for the return of the benchmark?

The answer is a resounding no.

In Chapter 6, I cited the studies of academic Michael Jensen, who did a thorough survey of the performance skills of mutual fund managers. The overwhelming majority of them underperformed the S&P 500. But he learned that many of them did so because the funds they managed held high percentages of cash.

That allowed the managers to argue that they were providing greater safety, if not greater returns. So Jensen then used sophisticated statistical methods to correct for the amounts of cash held. The majority still underperformed.

In fact, out of 115 funds, only 1 outperformed the market by more than 3% a year, while 21 underperformed by more than 3%. Of course, this was just one study, which was done more than 40 years ago. Certainly times have changed and active managers have gotten better, right?

Not so.

William Bernstein writes in *The Four Pillars of Investing*, "Since Jensen's study, literally dozens of studies have duplicated his findings and verified the last prediction: Past superior performance has almost no predictive value." In other words, just because a fund beat the market this year or over the past three years, it doesn't mean it's likely to beat the market over the next three years.

Of the few that do, it is often because of what is known as *style drift*. That means your fund manager is seeking better returns by straying beyond the fund's designated asset class—and undermining your asset allocation in the process.

Let's say, for example, that for your small-cap allocation you chose the mythical, actively managed Fidelity Super-Duper Small-Cap Fund. The fund's prospectus may well give the manager the flexibility to invest a substantial percentage of the fund's assets outside of the small-cap sector. The fund manager may be able to move money into mid-caps or even large caps. Maybe he or she can buy foreign stocks, or hold 25% in bonds.

In any given year, the fund may be investing fairly heavily in an asset class that performs better than small caps. As a result, the fund may wind up on the list of best performing small-cap funds. Temporarily. Because when this fund manager strays again from small caps but guesses wrong, as will eventually happen, the fund will move right back to the middle of the pack—the underperforming herd—or even worse, toward the bottom.

Meanwhile, what has happened to your disciplined asset allocation? It's been tainted. You may want to have 15% of your portfolio in small-cap stocks. But if your active small-cap manager is moving money elsewhere, you stand to miss the big rally in small caps when it comes. In essence, you end up missing the rally because your manager did.

Why take that chance?

Of course, not all superior fund performance is due to a fortuitous market timing call, or style drift. Some fund managers—an extremely tiny minority—show evidence of being superior stock pickers. Bill Miller at the Legg Mason Value Trust is one of them. He has beaten the S&P 500 by a significant margin since he took the helm in 1991. (Although he has stumbled lately, underperforming the market badly the past few years, his long-term returns are still well above average. He is a rarity.)

HERE TODAY, GONE THE NEXT

As we discussed in Chapter 4, truly talented fund managers are rare. (And many of the great ones, like John Templeton and Peter Lynch, left active fund management more than a decade ago.) Furthermore, fund managers who do show evidence of stock-picking skill have an unfortunate tendency to pick up and leave.

We live in an age where superstar money managers are treated like superstar athletes. In other words, they beat the market for a few years and are then given powerful monetary incentives to move around. So you may invest in a fund with a top-performing manager, only to find months later that he jumped ship.

I've often said that mutual funds don't have track records, fund managers do. Does it really make sense to buy, say, the Fidelity Magellan Fund due to its long-term track record?

Of course not. The man primarily responsible for its exceptional record, Peter Lynch, left the helm over 15 years ago. Many successors have since come and gone. To expect the fund to begin generating Lynch-like performance again is the triumph of hope over experience.

Of course, some funds are managed by a committee or use a specific strategy, like Value Line funds. Funny, though, you rarely see a fund managed by a committee winning any long-term performance awards. And, as for systems, most of them fail miserably, too.

Even the Value Line Fund, using the much-vaunted system published by the Value Line Investment Survey, has lagged the market by a substantial margin. So it behooves investors to understand that only a tiny minority of mutual fund managers demonstrate any evidence of skill.

In sum, the vast majority of mutual fund managers underperform their benchmark. Of the ones that do outperform, often it is due to style drift rather than stock picking. And since most of these are unable to maintain their streak, their success is more often attributable to luck rather than skill. Finally, the handful that stick to their style discipline and outperform their benchmark with consistency, tend to be mobile. Here today, gone tomorrow.

For all these reasons, the best fund company to implement the Gone Fishin' strategy, in my view, is Vanguard. Its funds are inexpensive, tax-efficient, and effective at capturing the performance of the asset classes in our portfolio.

The Four Biggest Investment Pitfalls

Furthermore, the Gone Fishin' Portfolio eliminates what I consider the four biggest investment pitfalls. Let me detail what they are and show you how our investment strategy avoids them:

1. *Being too conservative.* Investors who put their money to work exclusively in money markets, certificates of deposit and tax-free bonds generally think they're just being careful and sensible. But, unless they're already independently wealthy, they're not.

   The Gone Fishin' Response: The Roman philosopher Tacitus rightly observed that "the desire for safety stands against every great and noble enterprise." Invest too conservatively and you risk outliving your money, especially given today's life expectancies. According to the National Center for Health Statistics, at age 65, women can now expect to live, on average, another 19.2 years. The corresponding figure for men is 16.3 years. (These are just the averages. Many individuals will spend 30 years or more in retirement.)

   Remember, shortfall risk—the likelihood that you'll outlive your savings—is the biggest financial risk you face. Sure, no one wants to handle retirement assets foolishly. Yet being ultraconservative can be just that. Fortunately, our Gone Fishin' Portfolio contains 10 different asset classes—each of which is likely to outperform cash investments over time.

2. *Being too aggressive.* There are two reasons investors generally get too aggressive with their assets. One is that they're overconfident in their abilities or, in some cases, the abilities of their financial advisor. The other reason is that they realize they've fallen behind and have decided they're going

to get super aggressive with their investments to make up for lost time.

The Gone Fishin' Response: According to the 2007 Retirement Confidence Survey by the Employee Benefit Research Institute (EBRI), 36% of workers have less than $10,000 in retirement savings. Another 13% have less than $25,000. In other words, nearly half of all workers have less than $25,000 saved for retirement. That's unfortunate.

But if you haven't saved enough, it's highly unlikely your salvation will come in the form of options, futures, day trading, or margin accounts. Instead, investors need to spend less, save more, and use a realistic approach to growing their assets.

3. *Trying—and failing—to time the market.* As I mentioned before, it seems so easy when you imagine it: You'll be in the market for most of the run-up, and out of the market for most of the sell-off—then back in again for the next rally.

Except it doesn't work that way. What market timers invariably find, if they keep at it long enough, is that they're out during some of the good times and in during some of the bad times. The end result is high turnover (which leads to high costs), plenty of capital gains taxes, and substandard performance.

The Gone Fishin' Response: Yes, there are times when the market as a whole looks incredibly cheap, as it did in 1982. And there are times when the market appears awfully expensive, as it did in the spring of 2000. But the key to making money in the market is time, not timing.

However, there is a good living to be made offering market timing advice. So it shouldn't surprise you that "professional" market commentators don't see things the same way. I group these soothsayers into three categories: perma-bulls, perma-bears, and roadkill. Here's how they stack up.

Perma-bulls and perma-bears give strong opinions about where the markets are heading, but they are really not market timers at all. That is because they rarely—if ever—change their point of view. They are perpetually bullish or bearish.

Since the market has historically gone up three years out of four, perma-bulls, on the one hand, tend to be right most of the time. There's no shame, of course, in finding yourself owning stocks in a down market. That's simply part of the game. But by listening to a highly confident perma-bull, you may have more money invested in stocks than you're comfortable with—or might even be invested on margin.

Perma-bears, on the other hand, are forever seeing gloom and doom. They're wrong most of the time, of course, but during those periods when they're right, their warnings tend to echo in your ears. "Don't be a chump . . . a sucker . . . a fool . . . a patsy." Of course, whenever we do experience a genuine bear market, or even a minor correction, they're quick to remind you that they "told you so."

Unfortunately, no matter how low the market goes, these commentators are forever insisting that the bear market is just warming up. When the Dow dropped from over 11,000 in 2000 to roughly 7,200 in 2002, many perma-bears insisted it was still just the beginning of the end. Some of them, like Elliott Wave theorist Bob Precheter, were predicting 5,000 on the Dow—or less. Four years later, the market was up nearly 80%.

The last group—the true market timers—I call roadkill.

These are the timers who switch from bullish to bearish and back again. I've named them for the inevitable result of all their road crossings. (Think of the last opossum you saw that was shaped like a furry pancake.) It would be nice to think someone had this kind of clairvoyance. But as George and Ira Gershwin warned us, "It Ain't Necessarily So."

4. *Unwise delegation.* Delegators are investors who—fearful of being too conservative or two aggressive and rightly convinced they can't time the market—turn everything over to an insurance agent, planner, or full-service broker.

The Gone Fishin' Response: Unfortunately, brokers trade for commissions. Insurance agents sell some of the highest-cost products in the financial industry. And, over the course of several years, even planners will convert a substantial portion of your assets into their assets. Fortunately,

the Gone Fishin' Portfolio—which you can easily implement on your own—sidesteps the unwise delegation pitfall
altogether.

STICKING TO THE TRIED AND TRUE

The beauty of this system is that you'll never be out of the market
and therefore miss out on the kind of great returns that only stocks
have given over the long term. You will also never be fully invested
in stocks either, and take a drubbing as many investors did in the
savage 2000–2002 bear market.

Some will say that if you were fully invested in stocks and just
held on during this period, everything would have worked out
fine eventually. This is true, of course. But it neglects to take into
account human nature. We're reasoning animals, yes. But we also
tend to be motivated by fear and greed. Especially fear.

Very few individuals are stoic enough to watch their life savings
go through a slow motion, multiyear meltdown. The psychological pain becomes nearly unbearable. "There goes that cabin in the
mountains . . . There goes the membership to the golf club . . .
There goes early retirement."

And so they abandon hope and sell. Wall Street is the only
market where the customers don't buy when the merchandise
goes on sale. And there's practically always an asset class on sale
somewhere.

A balanced portfolio like this one is likely to decline less in
a market downturn. That makes you more likely to stick with
the program. When you rebalance your portfolio, you'll be taking
advantage of the fact that different assets classes move to the beat
of their own drummer. You'll be buying whatever is on sale.

When U.S. stocks are weak, for instance, foreign shares are often
rising. When both foreign and domestic stocks are down, bonds
generally go up. REITs move independent of most stocks and yet
have given excellent returns over the past 30 years. Junk bonds do
well in an economic recovery. Inflation-adjusted bonds will protect your purchasing power when consumer prices start to rise.
And gold shares act not only as an inflation hedge, but as an insurance policy against economic or political chaos.

Of course, the value of your portfolio will still fluctuate quite a bit. Some years will be better than others. And occasionally, you will see negative returns. That's unavoidable. It's also a good thing. Because it allows you to load up when an asset is cheap. Once a year—or every 366 days to avoid short-term capital gains taxes— you rebalance your portfolio, bringing each asset class back to its target allocation.

Essentially, you will evaluate your portfolio once a year and bring your assets back into alignment. This strategy of asset allocating and rebalancing has been battle-tested through all market conditions. It increases returns while reducing risk. It's so effective, in fact, that the idea won the Nobel Prize in economics in 1990. How many other investment strategies can make this claim?

That's why using a sensible asset allocation model—and rebalancing annually—is not just a priority. It's the safest, easiest, and best thing you can do with your serious long-term money.

But to earn the highest net return on your investments, you're going to need to take one other important step. You need to tax-manage your investment portfolio. That's the subject we'll turn to next.

REEL IT IN...

1. The Gone Fishin' Portfolio is a complete long-term investment program.
2. In addition to requiring little time and effort, it allows you to avoid the four most common pitfalls of investing: being too conservative, being too aggressive, trying—and failing—to time the market, and unwise delegation.
3. This strategy cannot promise positive returns every year. But your portfolio should do well in rising markets and will fall less than a 100 percent stock portfolio in a down market.
4. Much of the power and sophistication of this strategy results from an investment approach so successful it won the Nobel Prize in economics in 1990.

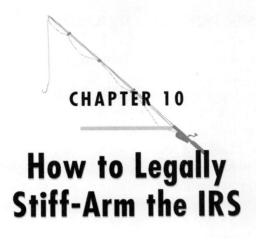

CHAPTER 10

How to Legally Stiff-Arm the IRS

"Be wary of strong drink. It can make you shoot at tax collectors—and miss."

—Robert Heinlein

We've already discussed the crucial importance of keeping your investment expenses under control. But there is another encumbrance that can do just as much (or more) damage to the long-term value of your portfolio. Taxes. As Arthur Godfrey said, "I'm proud to pay taxes in the United States; the only thing is, I could be just as proud for half the money."

If you're like most investors, there's a good chance you're paying more in taxes on your portfolio each year than you need to. So let's look at how you can keep your tax bite to an absolute minimum—and legally stiff-arm the IRS.

PRE-TAX VS. POST-TAX RETURNS

Mutual fund advertisements and the financial media love to tout funds' total returns. These returns take operating costs (expenses) into account, but not taxes. However, two funds with identical gross returns can deliver drastically different returns after taxes.

Mutual funds are required by law to distribute at least 90% of their realized gains each year. You can get hit with a big tax bill even if you haven't sold a share. How? Inside the fund, the manager may be buying and selling like mad, turning over the entire portfolio in less than a year. Although this doesn't necessarily hurt the fund manager's annual bonus, it can have a dramatic effect on your real-world returns. After all, you may owe taxes on all those short- and long-term capital gains, even if you haven't sold a single share.

Lipper, a global leader in fund information and analytical tools, recently published a study, *Taxes in the Mutual Fund Industry—2007: Assessing the Impact of Taxes on Shareholder Returns.* It found that taxable mutual fund investors surrendered at least $23.8 billion to Uncle Sam in 2006, just for buying and holding their funds! Taxes gobbled up 15% of the gross return of the average U.S. diversified equity fund. And the tax hit was even worse for the average U.S. taxable bond fund. Here, 38% of the gross return was lost to taxes, nearly double the cost of operating expenses and loads combined.

If anything, this study may have actually understated the tax costs. Why? Because it included the 2000 to 2002 bear market in stocks, so tax-loss carryforwards (and favorable changes in the tax code) actually mitigated the tax burden.

If you are voluntarily surrendering thousands of dollars to the IRS each year, it makes it much tougher to meet your long-term financial goals. For this reason, you need to tax-manage your portfolio to increase your real-world returns. Here's how.

THE TAXMAN COMETH

Your annual tax liabilities will depend, in part, on both your tax bracket and how much of your portfolio is held outside of qualified retirement plans. I'm going to run through a few different scenarios, allowing you to easily adopt the strategy that is closest to your own personal situation.

Let's start with the easiest scenario. If all your long-term money is in a tax-advantaged account like an IRA, Keogh, 401(k), 403(b), private pension plan, or annuity, you can stop sweating. You don't have to be concerned with the tax ramifications of your asset allocation and rebalancing strategy because you don't owe any annual taxes on the investments in these accounts. You're safe from the taxman until you begin making withdrawals. So if all your long-term money is in a qualified retirement plan—or at least the money you intend to use in the Gone Fishin' strategy—you can skip the rest of this chapter. You're already home free.

But, if you're like most investors, your personal situation is probably a bit more complex. You likely have liquid assets both inside and outside of retirement accounts. In that case, you'll need to do a bit of tax planning.

The first order of business is to place the appropriate funds in the right accounts for maximum after-tax returns. You'll need to put the most tax-inefficient funds into your tax-deferred accounts and the remaining funds in your taxable accounts.

For example, REITs are highly tax-inefficient. Most of your return will come in the form of dividends and these are taxable at your income tax rate, not the 15% capital gains tax rate. For this reason, the Vanguard REIT Index Fund should be one of the first things you place in your tax-deferred account.

Another tax-inefficient asset is high-yield bonds. Here the majority of the return comes from interest income—and all of it is taxable. A junk bond fund will typically make capital gains distributions from time to time, as well. So the Vanguard High-Yield Fund should also be placed in your tax-deferred account, if possible.

Also highly tax-inefficient are inflation-protected securities (TIPS). The semiannual interest payments on TIPS are taxable, the same as other Treasury securities. However, investors are also taxed on inflation adjustments to the principal, a situation that is commonly described as taxing *phantom income*. For these reasons, you should also hold your inflation-adjusted Treasuries in your tax-deferred account.

High-grade corporate bonds and ordinary Treasuries pay taxable income, too. They, too, should be held in your tax-deferred account, if possible. However, if you're running out of room in your retirement account at this point—and especially if you reside in an upper tax bracket—you should make a substitution here. Instead of buying the Vanguard Short-Term Corporate Bond Fund, invest in the Vanguard Intermediate-Term Tax-Exempt Investor Shares (VWITX). You'll get a slightly lower yield, but your dividends will be exempt from federal taxes. (If you reside in California, Massachusetts, New Jersey, New York, Ohio, or Pennsylvania, use one of the tax-exempt bond funds Vanguard offers for your state.)

Our remaining stock index funds are fairly tax-efficient, with one exception: small caps. If a small company is successful and keeps growing, it will reach the point where it is no longer a small-cap stock. (It will become large enough to be classified as a mid-cap stock.) As a result, it will eventually be removed from the small-cap index. When a small-cap index fund sells a small-cap stock, it will ordinarily generate a realized capital gain. That gain, of course, will be distributed to shareholders.

If you still have room in your tax-deferred account, own the Vanguard Small-Cap Index Fund (NAESX) there. If you don't, consider owning the Vanguard Tax-Managed Small-Cap Fund (VTMSX) in your taxable account. Again, this is especially important for investors who reside in the top tax brackets. However, long-term capital gains are currently taxed at a maximum rate of 15%.

In tax-managing your assets, it is important to put your high-yield bonds and REITs in your retirement accounts first. Why? Because these are the highest-yielding components of your portfolio and there is no tax-advantaged substitution you can make. There is no tax-free substitution for inflation-adjusted Treasuries, either. So plunk the Vanguard High-Yield Corporate Fund (VWEHX), Vanguard REIT Index Fund (VGSIX), and Vanguard Inflation-Protected Securities Fund (VIPSX) in your retirement accounts.

Our remaining funds—Vanguard Total Stock Market Index Fund (VTSMX), Vanguard Precious Metals and Mining Fund (VGPMX), Vanguard Emerging Markets Index Fund (VEIEX), Vanguard

European Index Fund (VEURX), and Vanguard Pacific Index Fund (VPACX)—are pretty darn tax efficient. These are fine for your taxable accounts. However, the Vanguard Precious Metals Fund (VGPMX) is not an index fund and may make occasional capital gains distributions. So if there is still cash available in your retirement account, you might own this there, too.

EVERYTHING IN ITS PLACE

I've talked a lot about the supreme importance of asset allocation. Tax managing your portfolio is essentially your asset "location" strategy. Ideally, you want to own your least tax-efficient assets inside your retirement account and your most tax-efficient outside them. Effective tax-management of your portfolio is critical and can dramatically increase your long-term, real-world returns.

Please don't think that this step isn't worth the trouble. It is. In April 2004, for example, Vanguard founder John Bogle gave a lecture at Washington State University where he pointed out that the average mutual fund takes 2.5% in annual costs each year. Taxes take another 2%, on average. No wonder the average mutual fund investor feels like he's on a slow boat to China. You can't reach financial independence as quickly if you're surrendering so much of your annual returns to the taxman and the mutual fund industry.

A brief illustration shows you why. Let's say one investor owns a $100,000 tax-managed portfolio of Vanguard mutual funds with an average expense ratio of 0.5%. Another invests the same amount, but is surrendering a total of 4.5% each year in taxes and expenses. Even if both portfolios have 10% gross annual returns, the results over time become dramatically different. (See Table 10.1.)

As seen in Table 10.1, the investor who keeps his taxes and expenses to a minimum ends up with a portfolio worth more than three times as much—and that's without generating gross returns that are any better! Clearly, if you're not doing everything possible to minimize your investment costs and taxes, you're at a serious disadvantage.

As a financial writer, I've written and spoken about this topic many times. Occasionally, this strategy provokes anxiety from some

TABLE 10.1 Effects of a $100,000 Tax-Managed Portfolio

Years	Tax-Managed Portfolio	Non–Tax-Managed Portfolio
5 years	$157,424	$130,696
10 years	$247,823	$170,814
15 years	$390,132	$223,247
20 years	$614,161	$291,775
25 years	$966,836	$381,339
30 years	$1,522,031	$498,395

investors who see tax-management strategies as an abdication of their civic responsibilities.

Nothing could be further from the truth. As a law–abiding U.S. citizen, you need to pay all the taxes you are obligated to pay—and not one penny more. As Judge Learned Hand, who served for years as Chief Judge of the U.S. Court of Appeals for the Second Circuit, famously wrote:

> Anyone may arrange his affairs so that his taxes shall be as low as possible; he is not bound to choose that pattern which best pays the Treasury. There is not even a patriotic duty to increase one's taxes. Over and over again, the courts have said that there is nothing sinister in so arranging affairs as to keep taxes as low as possible. Everyone does it, rich and poor alike, and all do right, for nobody owes any public duty to pay more than the law demands.

Amen, Judge.

Let me remind you, too, that our strategy is to wait at least a year and a day before rebalancing your portfolio. That means you will never be subject to short-term capital gains taxes, which can run as high as 35%. If you choose to rebalance your portfolio every 18 months, you can reduce your annual tax liabilities further, as you will only be creating a taxable event approximately every other year.

As Vanguard founder John Bogle has said, "Fads come and go and styles of investing come and go. The only things that go on forever are costs and taxes."

In short, taxes matter . . . a lot. Take the basic steps I've outlined here to tax-manage your portfolio and you're assured of higher real-world, after-tax returns.

REEL IT IN...

1. Voluntarily surrendering a significant percentage of your annual returns to the IRS each year makes it much tougher to meet your long-term financial goals.
2. Taxes can potentially be larger than your other annual investment costs combined. Studies show that typical investors surrender 2% of his annual return to the taxman each year.
3. Maximizing your real-world returns means tax-managing your portfolio to minimize the annual tax liabilities.
4. Implement an asset "location" strategy. Keep your tax-inefficient investments—such as bonds, REITs, and small-cap funds—in your retirement accounts. Keep your tax-efficient investments—such as large-cap stock index funds—in your non–retirement accounts.
5. If needed, substitute the Vanguard Tax-Managed Small-Cap Fund (VTMSX) for the Vanguard Small-Cap Index Fund (NAESX) and the Vanguard Intermediate-Term Tax-Exempt Investor Shares (VWITX) for the Vanguard Short-Term Investment Grade Fund (VFSTX).
6. Wait at least a year and a day before rebalancing. If you want to be even more tax-conscious, you can choose to rebalance every 18 months, further reducing your annual tax liabilities.

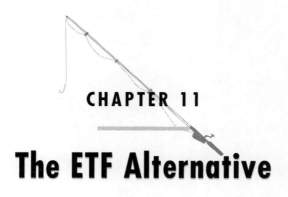

CHAPTER 11

The ETF Alternative

"Stay committed to your decisions, but stay flexible
in your approach."

—Tom Robbins

It's important to understand that the heart and soul of the Gone
Fishin' Portfolio is the asset allocation model, as we described in
Figure 7.1. (It is reprinted on page 138.)

In my view, the Vanguard Group is the best mutual fund company to implement this strategy because of its reliability and low
cost structure. However, if Vanguard funds are unavailable to you
for any reason, you can still replicate the Gone Fishin' Portfolio
using other fund families, providing they offer all 10 asset classes.
(Many fund groups do not.) Be sure it is a no–load fund family, so
your costs are kept as low as possible.

However, there are a couple of potential drawbacks to using
any mutual fund family, including Vanguard. As you know, a mutual
fund stands ready to redeem your shares on any business day, after

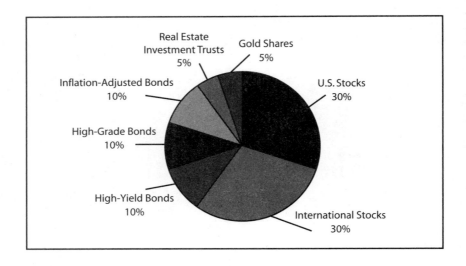

FIGURE 7.1 (repeated) The Gone Fishin' Asset Allocation

the market closes. Ordinarily, the cash for your redemption comes from fund inflows on the same day, the cash holdings of the fund, or the manager liquidating a small portion of the fund's holdings.

However, if a fund were to suddenly be hit with massive redemptions—due to a market panic, for example—the manager could potentially need to sell a large amount of securities to meet this demand. This might mean realizing substantial capital gains, even in an index fund. Since mutual funds are required to distribute these gains to shareholders each year, it could cause even a relatively tax-efficient index fund to suddenly become tax-inefficient (provided, of course, that you own these funds outside of a tax-deferred account).

Historically, the scenario I'm describing has not been a problem. But it never hurts to expect—or at least consider—the unexpected.

Another drawback, one that some potential Gone Fishin' investors have already experienced, is that the Vanguard Precious Metals and Mining Fund may close to new investors from time to time.

With gold moving sharply higher over the past few years, new money began piling in the door so rapidly that Vanguard didn't feel it could put the cash to work prudently. Since letting the cash stack up without putting it to work would create a drag on performance, Vanguard wisely chose to temporarily close the fund to new investors. (The entire global gold-mining sector, as I mentioned before, is only worth around $100 billion.)

As I write, this fund is not currently accepting new investments, with two exceptions. If you are a current shareholder of the Vanguard Precious Metals and Mining Fund, you are permitted to add to your holdings. Or, if you are a Vanguard Flagship customer— meaning you have more than $1 million in combined Vanguard accounts—you are free to invest in the fund. When the ardor for gold shares eventually wanes—as it will at some point—Vanguard will open the fund to new investors again.

In the past, when this fund has closed, I recommended the American Century Global Gold Fund (BGEIX), a similar no-load fund with a fine track record. But then, American Century Gold faced the same problem as the Vanguard gold fund, and eventually it closed, too.

With these two potential handicaps in mind, I'm going to offer an alternative version of the Gone Fishin' Portfolio. Our most important investment decision—the asset allocation—will remain the same. But the funds we use to implement it will be different. These funds will not close to new investors. They are even more tax-efficient than Vanguard mutual funds. And, in some cases, they have lower expenses than even Vanguard Admiral shares.

I'm talking about exchange-traded funds, more commonly known as ETFs.

MUTUAL FUNDS THAT TRADE LIKE STOCKS

ETFs are essentially mutual funds that trade on an exchange, like a stock. The first ETF was launched by State Street Global Advisors in 1993. The idea quickly caught fire. There are now hundreds of ETFs representing dozens of different market sectors and asset classes. (A recent update from the Investment Company Institute reported 560 funds trading in the U.S. with a total market capitalization of more than $550 billion.)

Here's what exchange-traded funds offer:

- Unlike ordinary mutual funds, which can only be bought or redeemed at the day's closing price, ETFs have an exchange listing and trade continuously throughout the day.
- They are linked to an index rather than actively managed (although the index itself may use an active rather than a passive strategy).
- Authorized shareholders can make redemptions on an "in-kind" basis, which means that rather than selling, shareholders can choose to receive large blocks of the underlying securities that make up the index in exchange for their ETF shares. (I won't go into the details here since this is not a part of our Gone Fishin' strategy.)

As you can see, ETFs offer several advantages. However, there are drawbacks to these funds, too. For example, the market price and the net asset value (NAV) of an ETF can diverge temporarily. This could be a problem if you wind up buying a fund at a premium to its NAV or selling it at a discount. (The NAV is used to determine the fair value of a security. It is calculated by taking the security's total assets, less liabilities, and dividing by the number or shares outstanding.)

However, two things keep the NAV and market price from straying too far apart. First, since the NAV is often quoted intraday, traders who spot the discrepancy can immediately buy or sell ETF shares to exploit the difference. In this way, self-interested investors keep the market prices relatively close to net asset values.

Also, as I mentioned, authorized participants can buy huge blocks of ETFs and trade them back to the fund for the shares in the underlying portfolio. These mostly large, institutional investors help ensure a relatively efficient market for ETFs.

Incidentally, I've had a few investors tell me that they avoid ETFs because of low trading volume. They are making the mistake of equating volume with liquidity. With ETFs, trading volume and liquidity are two entirely different things. Unlike closed-end funds, ETFs are open-ended.

This is an important distinction. Even without a change in the NAV, a closed-end fund can see a sudden dramatic change in the market price if there is a spike in trading volume. By contrast, a large number of buy or sell orders are unlikely to change the price of an ETF drastically, since new shares can always be created.

Also, because of their unique structure, ETFs can avoid the potential tax problem I mentioned earlier. When shares of an ETF are bought or sold, the transaction takes place on an exchange. In other words, the exchange, not the ETF's portfolio of securities, provides the liquidity. Mutual fund shareholders interact directly with the fund's portfolio when buying or selling shares. If a fund has big net redemptions, it could force the manager to sell securities, creating taxable pass-through gains to the remaining shareholders. The structure of ETFs is more tax efficient. You should experience little or no unexpected pass-through capital gains.

Moreover, ETFs are also wonderful for tax-loss harvesting at year end. One year, for example, you might be able to sell a broad market ETF, like the Vanguard Total Stock Market ETF (AMEX: VTI) at a capital loss and immediately replace it with another broad market fund, like SPDR DJ Wilshire Total Market ETF (AMEX: TMW). Even though there will be virtually no difference in the performance of the two funds—because they represent the same stock index (the Dow Jones Wilshire 5000)—the IRS does not disallow it, since they are two different securities.

WEIGHING THE ADVANTAGES OF ETFs

Clearly, ETFs have many benefits. And, fortunately, there is an ETF for every asset class in our Gone Fishin' Portfolio. For some investors, these ETFs will be more advantageous than traditional Vanguard mutual funds. For others, the Vanguard funds (or some other no-load group) are the better choice. Here's how to decide.

The first thing to consider in evaluating whether ETFs are right for you is the cost ratio. I've already written about the paramount importance of running your portfolio like Ebenezer Scrooge. Using no-load index funds instead of actively managed funds can cut your average annual costs from 3% to around 1.5%. By using Vanguard funds, you can lower them to around 0.25%. Using ETFs, however, you can halve even that amount to around 0.12%.

Still, there are a few ETF drawbacks to consider, too. Brokerage commissions, for starters. Trading an ETF is like buying or selling a stock. The order must be executed through a broker, so you are liable for a commission each time you place a trade. (However, if you're using an online or deep discount broker that commission may be $10 or less per trade.) There is also a bid/ask spread to cover with every publicly traded security, including ETFs.

These factors may seem relatively minor. But if you're adding money to your portfolio regularly, it can add up. At rebalancing time, too, some of your ETFs may need to be sold down and others added to, resulting in more transactions. Each time you add money to your portfolio or change its composition, you'll face commissions on the transactions.

No-load mutual fund companies like Vanguard, by comparison, will charge you nothing for transactions. They can also debit funds from your checking account each month and invest them for you automatically. If you were to invest monthly in the Gone Fishin' Portfolio with ETFs, paying even a $10 commission for each of the 10 funds, that's a $100 a month skim off of your investment or $1,200 a year. You can see that even small fees add up quickly.

ETF performance may also suffer slightly from a cash drag. When the stocks in an ETF portfolio pay a dividend, the fund pays those dividends out to shareholders periodically. But, until the pay date, that cash sits uninvested. Mutual funds, on the other hand, can reinvest the dividends immediately or pay them out to shareholders. This allows the capital to be deployed more efficiently. (ETF advocates often talk up the advantage of being able to buy ETFs intraday on a dip, for example. This is indeed a benefit for traders. But the Gone Fishin' Portfolio is not a short-term strategy, and intraday trading is not a factor for us.)

Clearly, both mutual funds and ETFs have their advantages and disadvantages. Deciding which to use depends on your particular situation.

The *Wall Street Journal* recently commissioned a study through Morningstar to figure out whether index mutual funds or ETFs are the better alternative. They found that mutual funds would provide a better return in 34 of 40 scenarios, outperforming by an average of 0.5% annually. And they didn't include the impact of commissions for ETFs. With these included, no-load mutual funds would have shone even brighter.

However, there are three specific groups of investors who could benefit from using ETFs:

1. Small investors who do not meet the minimum investment requirements for Vanguard or other no-load funds and who intend to invest through a deep discount broker annually or quarterly, not monthly.
2. Lump-sum investors who are putting most of their money to work up front and will be making few additional purchases, aside from the annual rebalancing.
3. Those who have most of their money in a brokerage account, don't want to move it, and have portfolios big enough to make the trading commissions moot.

THE GONE FISHIN' PORTFOLIO 2.0

For these investors, ETFs may be the best solution. Table 11.1 shows, for example, how you could construct the Gone Fishin' Portfolio using ETFs alone.

You'll find more complete information about each of these funds in Appendix B.

Please notice that the asset allocation is identical to the Gone Fishin' Portfolio as constructed with Vanguard mutual funds. In other words, I'm suggesting you own the same asset classes in the very same percentages. All we're doing is using ETFs instead.

As you can see in Table 11.2, however, the total annual expense ratio for this ETF portfolio is only 0.21%. That's rock bottom. (The total expenses for the Gone Fishin' Portfolio using Vanguard funds is approximately 0.25%.)

TABLE 11.1   The Gone Fishin' Portfolio 2.0: Exchange-Trade Funds

ETF	Symbol	Allocation
Vanguard Total Stock Market	VTI	15%
Vanguard Small–Cap	VB	15%
Vanguard European	VGK	10%
Vanguard Pacific	VPL	10%
Vanguard Emerging Markets	VWO	10%
iShares iBoxx High Yield Corporate Bond	HYG	10%
Vanguard Total Bond Market	BND	10%
iShares Lehman TIPs	TIP	10%
Vanguard REIT	VNQ	5%
Market Vectors Gold Miners	GDX	5%

Essentially, the choice is yours. You can create the Gone Fishin' Portfolio using Vanguard or other no-load fund companies. You can create it using ETFs in a discount brokerage account. Or you can create it using a combination of ETFs and mutual funds. (If the Vanguard Precious Metals and Mining Fund is closed, for example,

TABLE 11.2   The Gone Fishin' Portfolio: ETF Expenses

ETF	Symbol	Expense
Vanguard Total Stock Market	VTI	0.07%
Vanguard Small–Cap	VB	0.10%
Vanguard European	VGK	0.12%
Vanguard Pacific	VPL	0.12%
Vanguard Emerging Markets	VWO	0.25%
iShares iBoxx High-Yield Corporate Bond	HYG	0.50%
Vanguard Total Bond Market	BND	0.11%
iShares Lehman TIPs	TIP	0.20%
Vanguard REIT	VNQ	0.12%
Market Vectors Gold Miners	GDX	0.55%

you can buy the Market Vectors Gold Miners Fund—which will always remain available—and invest the rest in Vanguard funds.)

The important thing is this: Stick with the discipline:

1. Set up the initial asset allocation.
2. Keep taxes and operating costs to a minimum.
3. Rebalance regularly.

It's hard to think of an investment program much simpler than this. Or that allows you more time to go fishin'.

REEL IT IN...

1. Exchange-traded funds (ETFs) offer some benefits over no-load mutual funds, including potentially lower expenses and greater tax efficiency.
2. ETFs are available to purchase any day the nation's stock exchanges are open. Accordingly, shares of the Market Vectors Gold Fund ETF (AMEX: GDX) will always be available to new investors and can replace the Vanguard Precious Metals and Mining Fund, which may be temporarily closed.
3. ETFs also have drawbacks. These include the bid/ask spreads, commissions on all transactions, and the lack of some mutual-fund conveniences, such as instant dividend reinvestment, no-cost transactions, and automated purchases and withdrawals.
4. Vanguard funds are better for most investors, especially those making regular monthly purchases.
5. ETFs may be better suited for small investors who have less than $30,000 to invest (and therefore cannot meet the minimum investment requirements to hold the 10 Vanguard funds in the Gone Fishin' Portfolio); those with a lump sum to invest; or large investors whose portfolios are big enough to render transaction charges insignificant.

PART III

Get On with
Your Life

CHAPTER 12

The Last Two Essentials

Specific Goals and Realistic Expectations

"Goals are dreams with deadlines."

—Diana Scharf Hunt

Now that you understand what the Gone Fishin' Portfolio is and how it works, you may wonder if it will truly make you rich. That depends.

It depends on how diligently you save, how long you let your money compound, whether you rebalance regularly, and, perhaps most importantly, whether you have the discipline to keep from spending your fortune as it grows.

It also depends on your conception of "rich." The Oxford American Dictionary defines rich as "having a great deal of money or wealth." But then, how much is a great deal?

According to the latest statistics from the U.S. government, to be in the top 1% of U.S. households requires a net worth of $6 million. The minimum income required to be in the top 1% of American tax filers is $300,000.

But it doesn't take that much to be wealthy in the eyes of the Securities & Exchange Commission (SEC). This government agency is happy to give you a very specific definition of rich. You see, the SEC restricts hedge-fund ownership and other "private money" investments to wealthy individuals, who they assume can take care of themselves.

This requires the regulatory body to define—and occasionally redefine—what it means to be rich. On December 13, 2006, the SEC made a new ruling, saying investors need to have investable assets of at least $2.5 million, excluding equity in any homes or business, to be eligible for hedge fund ownership. That's a significant jump from the old standards, which required individuals to have a net worth of at least $1 million, including the value of primary residences, or an annual income of $200,000 for the previous two years for individuals or $300,000 for couples.

Forget keeping up with the Joneses. If you really want to consider yourself well off, now you have to keep up with the SEC.

Apparently, the federal government believes that, to be considered wealthy and sophisticated, having a million dollars just doesn't cut it anymore. The SEC, in its defense, claims it is just trying to keep up with inflation and booming asset prices.

Still, the SEC's new definition of rich—a net worth of $2.5 million (excluding home and business equity)—applies to only a small fraction of the American public. If you want to get there— or reach any other long-term financial goal—the Gone Fishin' Portfolio provides a tangible road map.

Yet, in my view, the quest for financial independence begins with having a clear, specific vision of where you are trying to go. As the old saying goes, for the ship without a destination, no wind blows fair.

TAKING AIM

For some people, a net worth of a few hundred thousand dollars is all they'd need to forget about money, relax, and enjoy themselves. Those who are interested in living the high life, or enjoying the finer things in life, will shoot for much more.

How much is *enough* is for you to determine, not me. But I have a few thoughts on how to make your dreams a reality. And it starts with having realistic expectations.

When I was in high school I was a low-handicap golfer. I lettered in the sport every year and alternated among the top two slots on the golf team during my senior year. However, it wasn't until I read Bob Toski's *The Touch System for Better Golf* (now out of print, unfortunately) that my game really started to improve.

Toski made a number of good suggestions, but one I found particularly helpful was his strategy for hitting off the tee. As a teenager, when I got ready to hit a tee shot, I simply aimed down the middle of the fairway and tried to hit it as far as I could without coming out of my shoes. (Plenty of other golfers, I've noticed, do pretty much the same thing.) Using this approach, I did hit the ball long, but too often it wound up in the elephant grass, not the fairway. That was costing me strokes.

Toski suggested that instead of just aiming down the middle and letting it rip, I should pick a specific spot in the fairway and hit to it as if it were a target.

The result? Instead of taking a "controlled wallop," I began swinging more within myself, much easier. And I couldn't argue with the results. I found the fairway a lot more often—and my score started coming down.

I think most investors would benefit from aiming for a target, as well. Too many investors simply plan (either consciously or unconsciously) to "make a whole bunch of money" or earn as high a return on their investments as they can. They're trying to hit it as far as they can—and that leads to all sorts of problems. You're likely to wind up in all sorts of speculative investments, like options, futures, penny stocks, or movie limited partnerships. The results are seldom salutary.

If you haven't been saving enough—or your investments haven't delivered a satisfactory return—it's unlikely your salvation will come from "taking a bigger swing." Yet many investors are susceptible to this temptation.

As a money manager, I once had a retired client who was sending money out of the country to invest in—of all things—a Mexican jojoba plantation. The investment syndicate was "guaranteeing" him returns of 28% a year.

This had scam written all over it, of course. But he trusted the individual he was dealing with—whom he'd only spoken to on the phone—and he received regular statements purporting that his money was indeed compounding at a 28% annual rate. So he was a true believer.

I argued that he should show some skepticism and investigate further—and, in the meantime, stop sending money overseas. Despite my arguments, he kept on. Finally, I suggested that he simply ask for part of his money back, as an act of good faith.

"But why would I want my money back," he asked, "especially when it's compounding at 28%? I should be sending even more."

Try it, I suggested. Something must have clicked because, eventually, he did. And, of course, he never saw a dime. Some readers will hear this story and say my client was duped, plain and simple. But he was duped because he had unrealistic expectations.

Instead of aiming for a reasonable target, he tried to just tee it high and let it fly. And, just like my errant drives, investments in penny stocks, movie partnerships, options, futures and Mexican jojoba plantations, generally end up in the weeds.

FINDING THE BULL'S-EYE

I can't overstate the value of having realistic expectations and a specific investment goal, something to shoot for. (Incidentally, the larger your portfolio gets, the more important this approach becomes.) To manage your "serious" money successfully, you need to aim at a specific target. You need a goal, a number. Without one, you may not get where you want to go.

Goals are dreams with deadlines. This is especially true in the case of financial dreams. Ideally, your financial goal should be clear and specific. It is not enough to say, "I'd like to have a lot of money some day." It is far better to say, "I intend to have $1 million on my 65th birthday." Now that's specific.

How you're going to get there should be quantifiable, too. For example, you can use a financial calculator to determine how to reach that $1 million goal.

Let's say that your goal is to accumulate $1 million from scratch over the next 25 years. Just visit www.easysurf.cc/vfpt2.htm and click on the link labeled *Savings Deposit—monthly deposit needed for a Future Value at term—interest compounded monthly.* It will show you exactly how much you'd need to set aside each month in order to achieve your goal.

To keep things simple, let's say, for example, the Gone Fishin' Portfolio returns 11% a year—the average return of the S&P 500 over the past 75 years. Saving and investing $634.46 a month each month—and letting it compound at 11%—will give you $1 million in 25 years.

Of course, the beauty of these calculators is that you can change the inputs to fit your personal circumstances. If you have more time before you retire—or less—you can adjust for that. If you aim to accumulate a larger sum, you can adjust for that, as well.

The important point is that you're more likely to achieve your goal if it's specific—and you know exactly what you need to do to achieve it. Of course, first you need to decide how much you need to retire comfortably. This is not always an easy task.

When I was growing up, a million-dollar net worth seemed unspeakably rich. Someone with that much money, I imagined, had no concerns about money whatsoever. (Presumably, he spent his whole day smiling, whistling, and counting his blessings.)

Today the situation is a little different. Yes, a million dollars is still a substantial sum. And by the standards of most of the world's population, millionaires are not just affluent. They are exceedingly wealthy. But I can assure you that most folks with a million-dollar net worth do not consider themselves rich.

According to the U.S. Census Bureau, in 2006 there were 9.3 million millionaires in the United States. That's 1 in 12 American households with a net worth of more than $1 million, excluding home values.

When I first read this, it came as a shock to me. However, at current interest rates, this sum conservatively invested in risk-free Treasuries will generate income of less than $45,000 a year. That's approximately the median household income in the United States. In an era of soaring housing costs, tuition, and health care, most people would not call a $45,000 income "living large."

But do you need to live extravagantly—or even want to? Think about it long and hard, and you may surprise yourself. If you truly enjoy your work, that's one thing. But for others, sacrificing so much time working for a bigger house, expensive cars, or fine things may be more trouble than it's worth. An affluent lifestyle makes it hard to save as much as you could otherwise—and also makes it tougher to drop out of the work force. It means the goal of financial independence is continually receding.

My favorite activities, for example, are tennis, hiking, swimming, reading, listening to music, and playing with my kids. The required annual cost of pursuing these interests—except for the occasional court fee and racquet stringing—is essentially zero. That has made it easy for me to live beneath my means and save regularly.

Someone whose interests lean more toward yachting, piloting their own plane, or collecting rare wines has a different perspective on the cost of hobbies. If you have the income to pursue these interests and still meet your financial goals, more power to you. But, for most of us, a simpler, less materialistic lifestyle could be the biggest liberating factor in our lives.

As Albert Einstein once wrote, "I believe that a simple and unassuming manner of life is best for everyone, best both for the body and the mind."

HOW TO CALCULATE YOUR "NUMBER"

Ultimately, it's up to you to decide what kind of lifestyle you want to live and how much income it will take to support it. But here's a quick and dirty calculation that financial planners use to determine how much you need to reach financial independence. Take your required annual income—apart from Social Security and any pension income you may receive—and multiply it by 25.

Want $50,000 a year? You'll need to accumulate $1.25 million. Need $100,000 a year? Make it $2.5 million. Need $200,000 a year? It's $5 million.

Why multiply times 25? Because a good rule of thumb, if you want to be conservative, is to draw down no more than 4% of your portfolio each year in retirement.

You should expect the annual return on the Gone Fishin' Portfolio to well exceed that, of course. But the returns above 4% will keep your portfolio rising in value, so that you get a cost-of-living increase over the years as you continue to make withdrawals.

Some financial advisors will argue that 4% is too conservative. They believe that takes into account too many worst-case scenarios where the market behaves badly or tanks just when you reach retirement. And they may be right. If they're wrong, however, you'll have taken a very bad gamble. You run the risk of *lifestyle relapse.* In other words, you may be unable to live in the style to which you've become accustomed.

For example, imagine drawing down your retirement portfolio while the stock market is in a multiyear tailspin. It doesn't make for restful nights. That's why 30% of our Gone Fishin' Portfolio is in various types of bonds, as well as REITs and gold shares, which are less correlated with the broad market.

So, yes, you can always draw down more than 4% of your investment in retirement. But the higher the percentage you take out, the greater the chances your portfolio will kick the bucket before you do.

How do you calculate that final sum you need to live on, your investment goal? In Lee Eisenberg's book *The Number,* he suggests the following approach:

A. Total up your invested assets
B. Multiply A by .04, which tells you how much annual investment income you might reasonably withdraw each year
C. Add in the annual value of any home equity you have (to do this, divide your total equity by the number of years

you expect to live. For example, if your age is sixty, and you have $400,000 in home equity, and expect to live to be one hundred, the annual value of your real estate would be $10,000)

D. Add any income you expect from any inheritance

E. Add the amount of Social Security you assume you're entitled to per year (for help, visit *www.sa.gov*)

F. Add any expected annual pension benefits

G. Add any remaining income you expect, such as from part-time work or other sources

H. Total B through G, and you arrive at how much you can safely spend through the rest of your life

I. Once you have this number, multiply by 25. That will give you "The Number"—the lump sum you're aiming to accumulate during your working years.

People are often shocked to find out how big this number is. Shocked because life is expensive—and it's easier to spend than to save. As Eisenberg writes, "Whatever you thought your Number was at age thirty will strike you as amusing by the time you're forty, a regular laugh riot at fifty."

Here's the good news, though. When you're in the accumulation phase, you may end up pleasantly surprised. As money compounds, it becomes the proverbial snowball rolling downhill. As I mentioned earlier, $500 a month compounded at 11% a year turns into more than $1.32 million in 30 years.

Of course, the focus of the Gone Fishin' Portfolio is to make sure your invested assets are doing the hard work required, so you can eventually leave your job—or do only work you enjoy—and live your version of retirement heaven.

The important thing is this. Knowing exactly what you want—and how you plan to get there—will go a long way toward helping you reach your target. Make your "number" realistic. Make it specific. And, most importantly, give it a deadline. That's how to turn your dream of financial freedom into a reality.

REEL IT IN...

1. Whether the Gone Fishin' Portfolio strategy allows you to reach your investment goals depends largely on your own fiscal discipline. How much you save, how long your money compounds, and whether you rebalance regularly are the key factors.
2. The quest for financial independence begins with having a clear, specific vision—with realistic expectations—of where you are trying to go. You're much more likely to achieve your goal once you know exactly how much is needed to retire comfortably.
3. Only you can determine how much money you'll need to achieve your dream retirement. But the more affluent your lifestyle, the harder it is to save money, which impedes the ultimate goal of financial independence.
4. Once you are retired, use 4% as a conservative estimate of how much you can draw down your retirement portfolio each year. This helps ensure your money lasts as long as you do.

CHAPTER 13

Your Most Precious Resource

"Time is but the stream I go a-fishin in."

—Henry David Thoreau

You are now ready to implement the Gone Fishin' Portfolio. Feel confident about your decision. This portfolio is based on decades of market analysis, as well as rigorous thinking about how to maximize your returns while keeping investment risk strictly limited.

The idea of diversifying broadly, asset allocating properly, cutting costs and taxes, and rebalancing annually may seem elementary. But simplicity is part of its charm, it's elegance. Moreover, there is no other strategy that comes closer to guaranteeing long-term investment success.

The Gone Fishin' Portfolio allows you to take your financial destiny into your own hands, and requires minimal time and effort. Putting this portfolio together is a snap. Maintaining it takes just a few minutes a year.

There are no guarantees the Gone Fishin' Portfolio has the best allocation for long-term growth. But no other system can guarantee it, either.

If an investment advisor tells you he has identified the single best asset allocation for the future, do yourself a favor. Run.

It's easy to look back and see which asset allocation was best for any given period. But we can never be certain in advance. Or, as William Bernstein writes in *The Intelligent Asset Allocator*, "Anybody who tells you their portfolio recommendations are 'on the efficient frontier' also talks to Elvis and frolics with the Easter Bunny."

You can look at historical data and examine what has worked in the past. But you cannot blindly extrapolate past returns into the future. If history could predict future returns, librarians would be the world's wealthiest people. Understand that there is no strategy—and no asset allocation decision—that guarantees you the best returns in the future.

History does teach us a number of important lessons, however. Over time, bonds return more than cash, but fluctuate in value. Stocks return more than bonds, but are more volatile still. And when you blend these noncorrelated assets together, including slightly more exotic fare like REITs, junk bonds, and gold shares, you are likely to capture excellent returns within an acceptable level of risk.

The pursuit of "the very best" asset allocation is not required to achieve your investment goals. What's more important is to develop a reasonable asset allocation—that includes a fair number of uncorrelated assets—and stick with your decision through thick and thin. That's what is paramount.

Saying it, of course, is easier than doing it. So I want to discuss a few of the psychological hurdles you're likely to face in the years ahead.

THE KEY TO LONG-TERM INVESTMENT SUCCESS

If a well-informed investor fails at managing his own money, the culprit is almost always the same: emotion. I call emotion "the enemy from within." Fortunately, the Gone Fishin' strategy helps overcome mental states like fear and greed, because this system emphasizes rationality and humility. We don't know what the markets are going to do next quarter or next year. Yet we have a discipline that allows us to capitalize on this uncertainty.

Still, in order to reap the rewards, you have to stand by your decision to asset allocate and rebalance, even when the headlines are trumpeting those four fatal words for investors: "This time it's different."

It's not.

The financial markets have experienced and survived inflation, recession, natural disasters, war, and depression. Stocks get knocked down, but they have always recovered. Investors begin to doubt this, however, whenever the black clouds appear on the horizon. Fear often trumps reason.

But you should heed the words of Daniel Goleman, the author who promoted the idea in the 1990s that success is more closely tied to emotional intelligence than education or knowledge. In his book *Emotional Intelligence,* he writes, "As we all know from experience, when it comes to shaping our decisions and our actions, feelings counts every bit as much—and often more—than thought . . . Passions overwhelm reason time and again." Unfortunately, passion is how great investment plans often come undone.

Goleman argues that two key aspects of emotional intelligence are impulse control and persistence. These are exactly the two qualities that will keep you from letting periods of poor market performance cause you to abandon your investment strategy in a panic.

In short, investment success is more often attributable to your EQ (emotional quotient) than your IQ. Here are four ways you can keep your emotions under control:

1. *Do a reality check.* Recognize that investing in stocks means your account value is bound to sustain wide fluctuations from time to time. It's unrealistic to think that you're going to earn the superior returns only stocks can give while watching your mutual funds rise as steadily as a savings account.

2. *Automate your investments.* If you're in the early stages of wealth accumulation, use a discipline like dollar-cost averaging—investing a consistent amount at regular intervals—to take advantage of the market's occasional swoons.

3. *Act unemotionally.* When you rebalance regularly, you check harmful emotions like fear, greed, hope, pride, or envy. Buying what everyone else is running from takes courage. But if you are equal to the task, you will be well rewarded.

4. *Sit on your hands.* Warren Buffett once said, "Inactivity strikes us as intelligent behavior." During volatile periods between rebalancing, you must resist the urge to "do something." It's one thing to feel fearful about the market. It's quite another to let that fear trump your well-laid investment plans.

Studies in behavioral finance clearly demonstrate that it's not your store of market knowledge that is most likely to determine your success as an investor. It's whether you let your emotions dictate your actions.

I'm not saying you shouldn't feel emotional from time to time. That would be asking too much. But if you let those emotions control your investment decisions, eventually you're going to feel something entirely different . . .

Regret.

This is not just my perspective, by the way. In *The Four Pillars of Investing*, William Bernstein writes,

It is not uncommon to meet extremely intelligent and financially sophisticated people, oftentimes finance professionals, who are still incapable of executing a plan properly—they can talk the talk, but they cannot walk the walk, no matter how hard they try.

The most common reason for the "failure to execute" shortcoming is the emotional inability to go against the market and buy assets that are not doing well. Almost as common is an inability to get off the dime and commit hard cash to a perfectly good investment blueprint, also called "commitment paralysis."

Most investors don't realize that their biggest obstacle to success is not inflation, or bad markets, the taxman, or Wall Street. As Benjamin Graham wrote back in 1934, "The investor's chief problem—and even his worst enemy—is likely to be himself." (Or, as the comic strip Pogo once put it, "We have met the enemy and he is us.")

The other pitfall, one that keeps investors from even getting out of the blocks, is procrastination. Many of us have big plans that—due to a lack of action—never get beyond the planning stage. Resolve that you will take responsibility for your success by understanding the timeless principles at work here—and move forward.

Don't make the mistake of waiting until the "right time" to get started. If all the stoplights had to turn green before you left home, you'd never get out of your driveway. By the same token, you'll never receive a sudden revelation that you have reached the perfect starting point for your investment program. There will always be troubles in the economy and challenges facing the stock market. But, as I have tried to emphasize throughout this book, the key to success in the market is time, not timing.

Look at Figure 13.1. It shows what your returns would have been had you had the ridiculous bad luck of buying into the market at its high point every year.

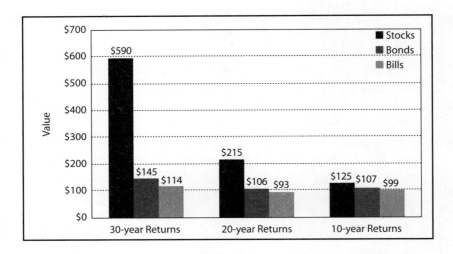

FIGURE 13.1 Average Total Returns after Major Twentieth Century Market Peaks

Note: Major Market Peaks include 1901, 1906, 1915, 1929, 1937, 1946 and 1968
Source: Jeremy J. Siegel, *Stocks for the Long Run*, 4th Ed., McGraw-Hill, 2007.

As you can see—and as I've been arguing virtually from page one—over the long haul, trying to time your entry point in the market is a mug's game. There is no bad time to start a disciplined long-term investment program. And, unless you've met your long-term goals—or reached that stage of life when you're ready to spend your fortune down—there is no good time to abandon it, either.

A PLAN FOR ALL SEASONS

Ultimately, the Gone Fishin' strategy is about waking up and taking the reins of financial freedom. You can't live your life fully if you're a slave to your job, your financial commitments, or your monthly overhead. Or, worse, if you're worried that you won't be able to maintain a comfortable retirement.

The essential truth of modern economic life is that money gives you choices. Chief among these is the opportunity to do what you want, where you want, with whom you want. That's what financial freedom is all about.

It's a shame, really, that more of us don't recognize this when we're young. But then, it's never too late to start learning—or to finish our investment education.

What will the Gone Fishin' Portfolio return in the future? The historical returns for each asset class in our portfolio are well known. It is reasonable to expect that they will be similar in the future. But certainly not in the short term. And perhaps not even over the longer term. Investing is always a challenge, and "the answer" is always qualified.

As Professor Siegel warns in *Stocks for the Long Run*, "The returns derived from the past are not hard constants, like the speed of light or gravitational force, waiting to be discovered in the natural world. Historical values must be tempered with an appreciation of how investors, attempting to take advantage of the returns from the past, may alter those very returns in the future."

No matter how thoroughly you understand historical asset returns and essential investment principles, it's important to realize that uncertainty will forever be your inseparable companion.

And that's okay. The Gone Fishin' Portfolio is a system that acknowledges uncertainty. Ultimately, it thrives on it. You understand that all asset classes go through up and down cycles. By investing this way, you'll always have a stake in whatever assets are performing best. And by rebalancing regularly, you'll keep buying low and selling high, preparing your portfolio for the next change in the cycle.

To gird you through the inevitable market declines—including serious bear markets—let me remind you of two important points:

1. *When you own a diversified stock portfolio, you own an interest in a broad selection of the world's biggest and most profitable companies.* If you take a moment to recognize, for example, that your holdings include a slug of Procter & Gamble, McDonald's, ExxonMobile, General Electric, and other high-quality companies, you're likely to sleep better and hang in there long enough for time to work its magic.
2. *Don't waste time looking at your portfolio too often.* Sure, it's fun to watch your account rise when times are good. But it does no good whatsoever to dwell on your portfolio's daily fluctuations in a market downturn, watching in anguish as your net worth declines—at least temporarily.

As a money manager, many of my clients would take a mental snapshot—if not an *actual* one—of the best statement they ever received. During market corrections, they would often remind me how much they had "lost in the market," failing to understand that nothing was truly lost unless they panicked and abandoned their equity allocation. They also apparently forgot that their account would never have reached that high-water mark if they hadn't been invested in stocks to begin with.

With an investment strategy like this one that is designed to last decades, you will see your share of bear markets. If it makes you feel better, remember that every one for the past 200 years was a long-term buying opportunity. Recognize this and it becomes tougher to believe that the next one is any different.

As an investment advisor, I tried valiantly to get clients to increase their exposure to stocks during market downturns. The ones who did prospered. But, for many, hanging on was all I could get them to do. Adding to assets that were down was often out of the question.

Of course, when times in the market were good, many assured me they would welcome the chance to buy in a downturn. That's when we were talking in the abstract. But when the bear market actually showed up, they sang a different tune. "I never imagined that 'this' would happen!" they'd say in frustration. And, of course, "this" is something different every time.

Yet history demonstrates that common stocks are nothing if not resilient. That's why I refer to them as "the great wealth-creating machine of all time."

Yes, the economy will suffer the occasional recession. And the market will stumble. Expect it. And remember that you're using a system that allows you to capitalize on these inevitable downturns. In fact, the odds are good that the long-term value of your portfolio will be greater because of them. After all, it's during down markets that you get an opportunity to buy what's cheap and prosper during the recovery that follows.

I'm talking rationally, however. Bear markets are emotional. They bring fear, loathing, and anguish. (After all, this is *real* money we're talking about.) But when these times come, recall that stocks give the highest long-term return because of the inevitable down periods you're bound to experience. In essence, you get paid to feel scared occasionally.

Understand that. Embrace it. And you're on your way to being a successful investor. Remember, there's nothing wrong with feeling scared when the market swoons on bad news. Just don't act on those fears.

Over the last 70 years, the average U.S. recession has lasted only 10 months. (You have to go back to the Great Depression to find an economic downturn that lasted longer than 16 months.) Enduring a downturn like this hardly requires superhuman resolve. And yet so many investors fail to do it . . . including professional money managers.

In a study published a few years ago in *The Journal of Portfolio Management*, Christophe Faugere, Hany A. Shawky, and David M. Smith—finance professors at the State University of New York at Albany—researched the performance of money managers who oversee pension funds, endowments, and high-net-worth accounts. Because most institutions work under strict investment guidelines, these academics were able to analyze performance based on different approaches to selling stocks.

The result? Institutional managers who fared best were those with restrictive rules that did not allow emotional decision making. The managers who relied on "flexible" sell strategies did far worse. Count me unsurprised. Institutional money managers are prone to rationalizing—and making emotional mistakes—just like amateurs.

And the culprit is virtually always either pride, ego, or emotion. As Greg Forsythe, director of the equity model development team at Charles Schwab, recently said, "Without any kind of sell strategy, emotions come into play. And emotions are almost always wrong."

Our Gone Fishin' strategy—if you follow it—enables you to check these reactions at the door. Expect the market to decline sharply sometimes. And abide by the one action you need to take each year—rebalancing—to take advantage of it.

To succeed with this strategy, only two steps are truly essential: a thorough understanding of the system, and the discipline to follow through. You have the strategy in your hands. You know what to expect. Now it's up to you to follow through.

TIME IS ON YOUR SIDE

As I've tried to make clear in these pages, genius is not the key to investment success. And neither is timing. Rather, it's patience and discipline.

However, the Gone Fishin' Portfolio is designed to deliver something even more important than superior investment returns. A reader who owns the portfolio once sent me the following note. The author is unknown.

> *Imagine there is a bank which credits your account each morning with $86,400, carries over no balance from day to day, allows you to keep no cash balance, and every evening cancels whatever part of the amount you had failed to use during the day.*

What would you do?
Draw out every cent, of course!
Well, everyone has such a bank. It's name is time.
Every morning, it credits you with 86,400 seconds.
Every night it writes off, as lost, whatever of this you have failed to invest
to good purpose.
It carries over no balance. It allows no overdraft.
Each day it opens a new account for you.
Each night it burns the records of the day.
If you fail to use the day's deposits, the loss is yours.
There is no going back. There is no drawing against tomorrow.
You must live in the present on today's deposits.
Invest it so as to get from it the utmost in health, happiness, and success.

Time, not money, is your most precious resource. It is the most valuable thing you have. It is perishable, irreplaceable, and, unlike money, cannot be saved. The beauty of the Gone Fishin' Portfolio is that it allows you to redirect your time to high-value activities, whether it's work you enjoy, time spent pursuing your favorite activities, or just relaxing with your friends and family.

In *The Pleasures of Life,* Sir John Lubbock writes, "All other good gifts depend on time for their value. What are friends, books, or health, the interest of travel or the delights of home, if we have not time for their enjoyment? Time is often said to be money, but it is more—it is life; and yet many who would cling desperately to life, think nothing of wasting time."

The Gone Fishin' Portfolio gives you an excellent opportunity to increase your wealth. But it *guarantees* you more time to devote to the people and pastimes you love.

Perhaps that is what recommends it most.

AFTERWORD

The Gone Fishin' strategy may be different from any investment portfolio you've owned or even considered owning. Yet the idea of asset allocating and rebalancing using low-cost, tax-efficient index funds is hardly unique.

As I made clear in earlier chapters there are good reasons to use mainly index funds.

This way, we don't have to worry about a fund manager's misguided attempts to time the market. We don't have to worry about picking the wrong stocks or holding too much cash. We don't have to worry about style drift. We don't have to keep checking to make sure the original manager is still at the helm. We know index funds are low cost and tax efficient. They take very little time to analyze and monitor. And they outperform the vast majority of actively managed funds.

However, I want readers to understand that I have serious philosophical differences with those asset-allocators who recommend index funds because they believe it is impossible to beat the market by selecting and monitoring individual stocks.

That's simply not so. I have beaten the market soundly with my own stock portfolio over the past two decades. I have done it for clients as an investment advisor. And I have done it with stock portfolios that I direct for The Oxford Club, as well. (The Oxford Club's investment portfolio has beaten the Wilshire 5000 Index by a margin of more than 3 to 1.)

I'm making this clear because I don't want readers to infer that I subscribe to the efficient market hypothesis (EMH), or its sister modern portfolio theory (MPT), whose followers also advocate index funds.

The efficient market hypothesis is the theory that all public information is immediately discounted into share prices by rational, self-interested investors. Therefore, its proponents argue, it is futile to try to outperform the market by selecting individual stocks.

EMH and MPT have much of value to say about risk and return, the benefits of diversification, and effective portfolio construction. But let's look at the basic premise of modern portfolio theory. We're all self-interested, yes. But rational?

Is a young woman thinking rationally when she marries the troubled guy who promises to change his ways and hew to the straight and narrow? Is a young couple thinking logically when they buy more house than they can afford so they can live up to a certain image of success? Is a balding, middle-aged man thinking rationally when he plunks down hard cash for an expensive convertible to impress women half his age?

Perhaps not.

You may want to read Michael Shermer's excellent book *The Mind of the Market*. Shermer, a columnist for *Scientific American* and the founder of *Skeptic* magazine writes, "We are remarkably irrational creatures, driven as much (if not more) by deep and unconscious emotions that evolved over the eons as we are by logic and conscious reason developed in the modern world."

He backs up this claim with plenty of examples from the new science of behavioral economics. Studies show, for example, that most people are willing to drive five blocks if they can buy a $100 cell phone for half price. But they are far less willing to drive five blocks to save $50 on a $1,000 plasma TV. Why? After all, fifty bucks is fifty bucks, no matter how you spend it—or save it. But, according to Shermer, *mental accounting* makes us reluctant to make the effort to save money when the relative amount we're dealing with is small.

Or take the *sunk-cost* fallacy. Objectively, a company with lousy business prospects is not worth holding, no matter what you paid for it. Yet many investors will hold on to a losing stock for years, even when it's clearly unprofitable. Shermer correctly points out, "Rationally, we should just compute the odds of succeeding from this point forward." Yet investors who have sunk a lot into a stock—including a fair amount of ego—have trouble doing this.

Mental accounting and the sunk-cost fallacy are just the tip of the iceberg. Shermer shows that consumers and investors also fall prey to cognitive dissonance, hindsight bias, self-justification, inattentional blindness, confirmation bias, the introspection illusion, the availability fallacy, self-serving bias, the representative fallacy, the law of small numbers, attribution bias, the low aversion effect, framing effects, the anchoring fallacy, the endowment effect, and blind spot bias. (And you thought most of us only had a couple small glitches upstairs.)

By the time Shermer is done exposing all the flaws in our mental machinery, you feel inclined to put the efficient market hypothesis right up there with the "stork theory" in sex education.

Okay, I'm exaggerating . . . a little. Every experienced investor knows that shares of most publicly traded companies are fairly efficiently priced most of the time. But that's a whole lot different than saying *all* shares are efficiently priced *all* of the time, the foundation stone of efficient market theory.

Warren Buffett summed up my view nicely—if not entirely accurately—when he once remarked, "I'd be a bum on the street with a tin cup if the markets were always efficient."

I make this distinction because EMH proponents often point to much of the same data I've used about the poor performance of actively managed mutual funds. But as we've seen, there are plenty of reasons—many of them related to operating costs, cash holdings, and blinkered attempts to time the market—that cause actively managed funds to founder in their quest to beat their benchmarks.

It's true that the stock market is efficient at absorbing and discounting news and opinions. But that doesn't mean that attractive buying opportunities don't develop with individual stocks. If this were strictly true, no investment strategy would be better than a coin toss.

Yet that's exactly what hard-core EMH and MPT advocates argue. Listen to just a few of the EMH proponents that I've quoted favorably throughout the book:

- In *What Wall Street Doesn't Want You to Know*, Larry Swedroe writes that "current market prices reflect the total knowledge and expectations of all investors and no one can know more than the market does collectively."
- In *The Intelligent Asset Allocator*, William Bernstein writes that "mutual fund manager performance does not persist and the return of stock picking is zero."
- In *The Coffeehouse Investor*, Bill Schulthesis writes that "any attempt to beat the market is likely to prove disastrous to your long-term financial health."

Efficient market advocates begrudgingly acknowledge a few famous investors who have beaten the market over a period of decades. But they rationalize that if enough money managers try to beat the market, the law of averages says a lucky handful will succeed over the long haul.

By this reasoning, Warren Buffett is just one of the 1 in 23 million guys who bought the right lottery ticket. But that's absurd. Buffett is a financial genius who has forgotten more about successful stock picking than most investment analysts will ever know.

The MPT'ers do have it partially right. You're not going to beat the market over the long haul by trying to guess what the market's likely to do next. But to say you can't beat the market through superior stock selection is naive.

Don't get me wrong. I'm not saying it's easy. It's not. It requires knowledge, discipline, and, sometimes, nerves of steel. But it's certainly possible.

Yes, the overwhelming majority of active fund managers do fail to beat the market. But as an individual investor trading for your own account, you don't have the same handicaps they do.

For starters, you are not managing an enormous sum of money, hundreds of millions or billions of dollars. You do not have to worry about the market-impact cost of your trades. You do not face the pressures not to disappoint your clients with this quarter's results. You do not have to pay Wall Street specialists to accumulate or unwind your positions. And you do not have to deduct active-management fees from your returns.

Having said this, I'm ready to concede that beating the market over the long haul is harder than it looks—and many if not most amateur investors will fail. Still, for those investors who truly enjoy hunting big game and enjoy devoting the hours required to become good at selecting stocks, there is no reason to be pessimistic.

Allow me a few caveats, however.

I learned most of my investment lessons the hard way. And they took years to sink in. Plenty of individual stock traders—even ones that wind up doing well—report similar experiences. It may be possible to learn how to trade stocks by simply reading a book or listening to someone else's experience, but I've never met anyone who's actually done it.

When it comes to investing in individual stocks, the only lessons that stick, it seems, are those that come with a kick in the pants.

Fortunately, I learned most of them when I was investing relatively small sums. And I was young enough that I had plenty of time to make up for my mistakes. The older and closer to financial independence you are, the less attractive this path becomes.

Remember, too, I worked in the financial industry, spending thousands of hours watching knowledgeable traders, reading, studying the great investors, and practicing what I learned.

Most people don't have this kind of time to devote to stock picking. And, even if they do, there's no guarantee they will get the results they're seeking. Sometimes all they get is an expensive education.

So how have I been able to select stock ideas that earn higher-than-average returns? That would take another book. And, even then, I'm not sure I could explain it all.

Being a successful investor takes experience. It means comprehending business and the economy. It means understanding human psychology. But a large part, perhaps the biggest part of all, is temperament. Successful trading takes patience, fortitude, and the ability to withstand temporary—and sometimes permanent—losses.

Obviously, there is a lot more to selecting stocks than I can relate in a few pages here. If you're interested in trading individual stocks, you can subscribe to the *Oxford Club Communique,* the investment letter that I direct. Or you can read my market commentary for free at InvestmentU.com.

Of course, modern portfolio theorists will claim that my personal winning streak—and my investment letter's—are due to luck, not skill. Fine. We keep beating the market. They keep calling me lucky.

I hope nothing ever changes.

APPENDIX A

Vanguard Funds*

VANGUARD TOTAL STOCK MARKET INDEX

Overview

Symbol	VTSMX
Expense Ratio	0.15%
Inception Date	4/27/1992
Yield	1.93%
Admiral Shares	VTSAX

Description

The fund employs a passive management—or indexing—investment approach designed to track the performance of the MSCI U.S. Broad Market Index, which represents 99.5% or more of the total market capitalization of all of the U.S. common stocks regularly traded on the New York and American Stock Exchanges, and the Nasdaq over-the-counter market. The fund typically holds the largest 1,200 to 1,300 stocks in its target index (covering nearly 95% of the index's total market capitalization) and a representative sample of the remaining stocks. The fund holds a range of securities that, in the aggregate, approximates the full index in terms of key characteristics. These key characteristics include industry weightings and market capitalization, as well as certain financial measures, such as price/earnings ratio and dividend yield.

Performance

TABLE A.1   After-Tax Returns—as of 03/31/2008

	1 Year	3 Year	5 Year	10 Year	Since Inception 04/27/1992
Total Stock Market Index Inv					
Returns before Taxes	−5.79%	6.19%	12.27%	3.89%	9.67%
Returns after Taxes on Distributions	−6.04%	5.92%	12.00%	3.47%	9.01%
Returns after Taxes on Distributions and Sale of Fund Shares	−3.40%	5.31%	10.73%	3.18%	8.36%
Average Large Blend Fund					
Returns before Taxes	−5.13%	5.69%	11.15%	3.60%	—
Returns after Taxes on Distributions	—	—	—	—	—
Returns after Taxes on Distributions and Sale of Fund Shares	—	—	—	—	—

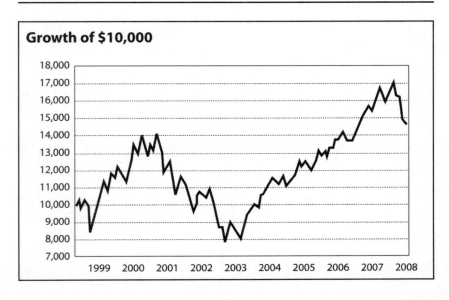

Holdings

Number of Holdings	3552
Total Net Assets	$100.6 billion

Top Ten Holdings

- ExxonMobil Corp
- General Electric Co.
- Microsoft Corp.
- AT&T Inc.
- The Procter & Gamble Co.
- Chevron Corp.
- Johnson & Johnson
- Bank of America Corp.
- International Business Machines Corp.
- Altria Group, Inc.

Risk Attributes

TABLE A.2 Historic Volatility Measures

Benchmark	R-squared*	Beta*
Spliced Total Stock Market Index	1.00	1.00
Dow Jones Wilshire 5000 Composite Index	1.00	0.99

*R-squared and beta are calculated from trailing 36-month fund returns relative to the associated benchmark.

Management

Gerard C. O'Reilly, Principal

- Portfolio manager
- Advised the fund since 1994
- Worked in investment management since 1992
- B.S., Villanova University

Investment Policy

The fund reserves the right to invest, to a limited extent, in stock futures and options contracts, warrants, convertible securities, and swap agreements, which are types of derivatives. It may use these investments for two reasons: to keep cash on hand to meet share-holder redemptions or other needs while simulating full investment in stocks or to reduce costs by buying futures instead of actual stocks when futures are cheaper. Losses (or gains) involving futures and options contracts can be substantial—in part because a relatively small price movement in a contract may result in an immediate and substantial loss (or gain) for the fund. Similar risks exist for warrants, convertible securities, and swap agreements. For this reason, the fund will not use such investments for speculative purposes.

Who Should Invest
- Investors seeking the broadest exposure to the U.S. stock market
- Investors with a long-term investment horizon (at least five years)

Who Should Not Invest
- Investors unwilling to accept significant fluctuations in share price
- Investors seeking significant dividend income

Minimums

TABLE A.3 Minimums

	Initial Minimum	Additional Investments
General Account	$3,000	$100
IRA	$3,000	$100
UGMAs/UTMAs	$3,000	$100
Education Savings Account	$2,000	$100

Expenses

TABLE A.4 Expenses

	Expense Ratio
Vanguard Total Stock Market Index Inv	0.15%
Average Large Blend Fund	1.18%

How Costs Affect Returns Over Time

$26,809

$24,169

The impact on a $10,000 investment with a 10.53% annual rate of return over 10 years.

VANGUARD SMALL-CAP INDEX FUND

Overview

Symbol	NAESX
Expense Ratio	0.22%
Inception Date	10/3/1960
Yield	1.49%
Admiral Shares	VSMAX

Description

The fund employs a passive management—or indexing—investment approach designed to track the performance of the MSCI® U.S. Small-Cap 1750 Index, a broadly diversified index of stocks of smaller U.S. companies. The fund attempts to replicate the target index by investing all, or substantially all, of its assets in the stocks that make up the index, holding each stock in approximately the same proportion as its weighting in the index.

TABLE A.5 After-Tax Returns—Updated Quarterly as of 03/31/2008

	1 Year	3 Year	5 Year	10 Year	Since Inception 10/03/1960
Small–Cap Index Fund Inv					
Returns before Taxes	−11.24%	5.84%	15.84%	5.70%	10.71%
Returns after Taxes on Distributions	−11.47%	5.60%	15.59%	4.64%	—
Returns after Taxes on Distributions and Sale of Fund Shares	7.11%	4.95%	13.90%	4.38%	—
Average Small Blend Fund					
Returns before Taxes	−13.29%	4.47%	14.63%	6.21%	—
Returns after Taxes on Distributions	—	—	—	—	—
Returns after Taxes on Distributions and Sale of Fund Shares	—	—	—	—	—

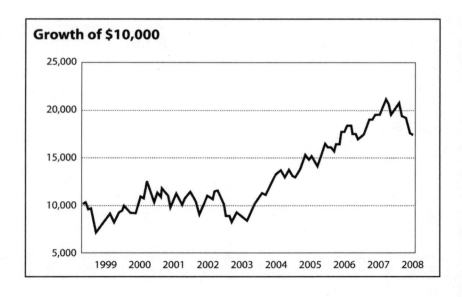

Holdings

Number of Holdings	1727
Total Net Assets	$13.5 billion

Top Ten Holdings

- Cleveland–Cliffs Inc.
- Cabot Oil & Gas Corp.
- Helmerich & Payne, Inc.
- Priceline.com, Inc.
- FMC Corp.
- Terra Industries, Inc.
- Illumina, Inc.
- Forest Oil Corp.
- Reliance Steel & Aluminum Co.
- Bucyrus International, Inc.

Risk Attributes

TABLE A.6 Historic Volatility Measures as of 03/31/2008

Benchmark	R-squared*	Beta*
Spliced Small–Cap Index	1.00	1.00
Dow Jones Wilshire 5000 Composite Index	0.86	1.29

*R-squared and beta are calculated from trailing 36-month fund returns relative to the associated benchmark.

Management

Michael H. Buek, CFA, Principal

- Portfolio manager
- Advised the fund since 1991
- Worked in investment management since 1987
- B.S., University of Vermont
- M.B.A., Villanova University

Investment Policy

The fund reserves the right to invest, to a limited extent, in stock futures and options contracts, warrants, convertible securities, and swap agreements, which are types of derivatives. It may use these investments for two reasons: to keep cash on hand to meet shareholder redemptions or other needs while simulating full investment in stocks, and to reduce costs by buying futures instead of actual stocks when futures are cheaper. Losses (or gains) involving futures and options contracts can be substantial—in part, because a relatively small price movement in a contract may result in an immediate and substantial loss (or gain) for the fund. Similar risks exist for warrants, convertible securities, and swap agreements. For this reason, the fund will not use such investments for speculative purposes.

Who Should Invest

- Investors seeking a simple, low-cost way to invest in small-capitalization stocks
- Investors with a long-term investment horizon (at least five years)

Who Should Not Invest

- Investors unwilling to accept significant fluctuations in share price
- Investors seeking significant dividend income

Minimums

TABLE A.7 Minimums

	Initial Minimum	Additional Investments
General Account	$3,000	$100
IRA	$3,000	$100
UGMAs/UTMAs	$3,000	$100
Education Savings Account	$2,000	$100

Expenses

TABLE A.8 Expenses

	Expense Ratio
Vanguard Small-Cap Index Fund Inv	0.22%
Average Small Blend Fund	1.44%

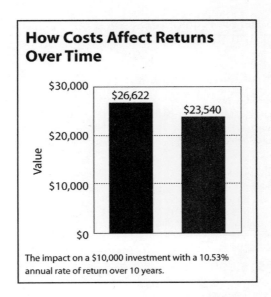

How Costs Affect Returns Over Time

The impact on a $10,000 investment with a 10.53% annual rate of return over 10 years.

VANGUARD EUROPEAN STOCK INDEX FUND

Overview

Symbol	VEURX
Expense Ratio	0.22%
Inception Date	6/18/1990
Yield	n/a
Admiral Shares	VEUSX

Description

The fund employs a passive management—or indexing—investment approach by investing all, or substantially all, of its assets in the common stocks included in the MSCI Europe Index. The MSCI Europe Index is made up of common stocks of companies located in 16 European countries—mostly companies in the United Kingdom, France, Switzerland, and Germany. Other countries represented in the index include Austria, Belgium, Denmark, Finland, Greece, Ireland, Italy, the Netherlands, Norway, Portugal, Spain, and Sweden.

TABLE A.9   After-Tax Returns—Updated Quarterly as of 03/31/2008

	1 Year	3 Year	5 Year	10 Year	Since Inception 06/18/1990
European Stock Index Inv					
Returns Before Taxes	−0.02%	14.76%	22.89%	6.67%	10.18%
Returns After Taxes on Distributions	−0.47%	14.31%	22.40%	6.07%	9.52%
Returns After Taxes on Distributions and Sale of Fund Shares	0.66%	12.76%	20.31%	5.55%	8.90%
Average Europe Stock Fund					
Returns Before Taxes	−1.20%	15.96%	24.48%	9.68%	—
Returns After Taxes on Distributions	—	—	—	—	—
Returns After Taxes on Distributions and Sale of Fund Shares	—	—	—	—	—

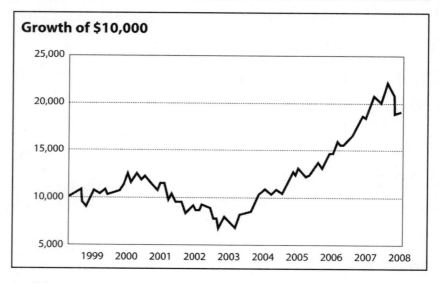

Holdings

Number of Holdings   634
Total Net Assets $33.4 billion

Top Ten Holdings

- BP PLC
- Nestle SA
- HSBC Holdings PLC
- Vodafone Group PLC
- Total SA

- Nokia Oyj
- Roche Holdings AG
- Telefonica SA
- GlaxoSmithKline PLC
- E.On AG

Risk Attributes

TABLE A.10 Historic Volatility Measures as of 03/31/2008

Benchmark	R-squared*	Beta*
MSCI Europe Index	0.97	0.96
MSCI AC World Index ex USA	0.86	0.84

*R-squared and beta are calculated from trailing 36-month fund returns relative to the associated benchmark.

Management

Duane F. Kelly, Principal

- Portfolio manager
- Advised the fund since 1992
- Worked in investment management since 1989
- B.S., La Salle University

Investment Policy

The fund may invest in derivatives, including futures and options contracts. These contracts may be used to keep cash on hand to meet shareholder redemptions while simulating investment in stocks, to make trading easier, or to reduce costs by buying futures instead of actual stocks when futures are cheaper. Losses (or gains) involving futures and options contracts can be substantial—in part, because a relatively small price movement in a contract may result in an immediate and substantial loss (or gain) for the fund. Similar risks exist for warrants, convertible securities, and swap agreements. For this reason, the fund will not use such investments for speculative purposes.

The fund may enter into forward currency contracts and foreign futures contracts to maintain the same currency exposure as its target index. However, the fund will not use these contracts to speculate or to hedge against currency fluctuations.

To earn additional income, the fund may lend its investment securities to qualified institutional investors.

Who Should Invest

- Investors seeking to further diversify a portfolio of U.S. securities
- Investors seeking long-term growth of capital
- Investors with a long-term investment horizon (at least five years)

Who Should Not Invest

- Investors unwilling to accept significant fluctuations in share price
- Investors seeking significant dividend income

Minimums

TABLE A.11   Minimums

	Initial Minimum	Additional Investments
General Account	$3,000	$100
IRA	$3,000	$100
UGMAs/UTMAs	$3,000	$100
Education Savings Account	$2,000	$100

Expenses

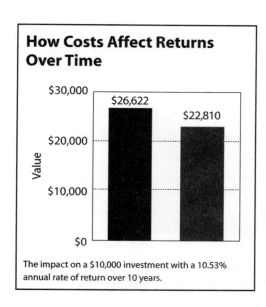

How Costs Affect Returns Over Time

The impact on a $10,000 investment with a 10.53% annual rate of return over 10 years.

TABLE A.12 Expenses

	Expense Ratio
Vanguard European Stock Index Inv	0.22%
Average Europe Stock Fund	1.75%

VANGUARD PACIFIC STOCK INDEX FUND

Overview

Symbol	VPACX
Expense Ratio	0.22%
Inception Date	6/18/1990
Yield	n/a
Admiral Shares	VPADX

Description

The fund employs a passive management—or indexing—investment approach by investing all, or substantially all, of its assets in the common stocks included in the MSCI Pacific Index. The MSCI

TABLE A.13 After-Tax Returns—Updated Quarterly as of 03/31/2008

	1 Year	3 Year	5 Year	10 Year	Since Inception 06/18/1990
Pacific Stock Index Inv					
Returns before Taxes	−7.87%	10.39%	18.15%	5.35%	2.13%
Returns after Taxes on Distributions	−8.31%	9.95%	17.72%	5.00%	1.81%
Returns after Taxes on Distributions and Sale of Fund Shares	−4.76%	8.85%	15.93%	4.51%	1.68%
Average Japan Stock Fund					
Returns before Taxes	−17.98%	3.19%	12.66%	3.53%	—
Returns after Taxes on Distributions	—	—	—	—	—
Returns after Taxes on Distributions and Sale of Fund Shares	—	—	—	—	—

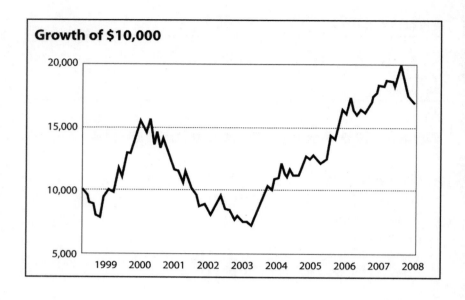

Growth of $10,000

Pacific Index consists of common stocks of companies located in Japan, Australia, Hong Kong, Singapore, and New Zealand.

Holdings

Number of Holdings	590
Total Net Assets	$15.3 billion

Top Ten Holdings

- Toyota Motor Corp.
- BHP Billiton Ltd.
- Mitsubishi UFJ Financial Group
- Commonwealth Bank of Australia
- Nintendo Co.
- Canon, Inc.
- Honda Motor Co., Ltd.
- Sumitomo Mitsui Financial Group, Inc.
- Sony Corp.
- Takeda Pharmaceutical Co. Ltd.

Risk Attributes

TABLE A.14 Historic Volatility Measures as of 03/31/2008

Benchmark	R-squared*	Beta*
MSCI Pacific Index	0.94	0.95
MSCI AC World Index ex USA	0.68	0.79

*R-squared and beta are calculated from trailing 36-month fund returns relative to the associated benchmark.

Management

Michael H. Buek, CFA, Principal

- Portfolio manager
- Advised the fund since 1997
- Worked in investment management since 1987
- B.S., University of Vermont
- M.B.A., Villanova University

Investment Policy

The fund may invest in derivatives, including futures and options contracts. These contracts may be used to keep cash on hand to meet shareholder redemptions while simulating investment in a market index, to make trading easier, or to reduce costs by buying futures instead of actual stocks when futures are cheaper. Losses (or gains) involving futures and options contracts can be substantial—in part because a relatively small price movement in a contract may result in an immediate and substantial loss (or gain) for the fund. Similar risks exist for warrants, convertible securities, and swap agreements. For this reason, the fund will not use such investments for speculative purposes.

The fund may enter into forward currency contracts and foreign futures contracts to maintain the same currency exposure as its target index. However, the fund will not use these contracts to speculate or to hedge against currency fluctuations.

To earn additional income, the fund may lend its investment securities to qualified institutional investors.

Who Should Invest

- Investors seeking to further diversify a portfolio of U.S. securities
- Investors seeking long-term growth of capital
- Investors with a long-term investment horizon (at least five years)

Who Should Not Invest

- Investors unwilling to accept significant fluctuations in share price
- Investors seeking significant dividend income

Minimums

TABLE A.15 Minimums

	Initial Minimum	Additional Investments
General Account	$3,000	$100
IRA	$3,000	$100
UGMAs/UTMAs	$3,000	$100
Education Savings Account	$2,000	$100

Expenses

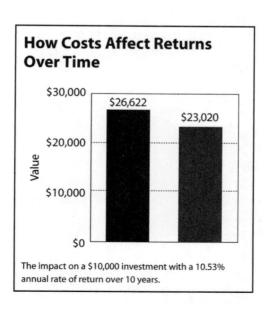

How Costs Affect Returns Over Time

$26,622

$23,020

The impact on a $10,000 investment with a 10.53% annual rate of return over 10 years.

TABLE A.16 Expenses

	Expense Ratio
Vanguard Pacific Stock Index Inv	0.22%
Average Japan Stock Fund	1.66%

VANGUARD EMERGING MARKETS STOCK INDEX FUND

Overview

Symbol	VEIEX
Expense Ratio	0.37%
Inception Date	5/4/1994
Yield	n/a
Admiral Shares	VEMAX

Description

The fund employs a passive management—or indexing—investment approach by investing substantially all (normally about 95%) of its assets in the common stocks included in the MSCI Emerging

TABLE A.17 After-Tax Returns—Updated Quarterly as of 03/31/2008 (fee-adjusted)

	1 Year	3 Year	5 Year	10 Year	Since Inception 05/04/1994
Emerging Markets Stock Index Inv					
Returns before Taxes	20.49%	27.53%	34.70%	12.96%	10.15%
Returns after Taxes on Distributions	20.14%	27.22%	34.38%	12.36%	9.57%
Returns after Taxes on Distributions and Sale of Fund Shares	13.78%	24.10%	31.33%	11.27%	8.78%
Average Diversified Emerging Markets Fund					
Returns before Taxes	17.92%	27.48%	33.73%	11.98%	—
Returns after Taxes on Distributions	—	—	—	—	—
Returns after Taxes on Distributions and Sale of Fund Shares	—	—	—	—	—

Markets Index while employing a form of index sampling to reduce risk. The MSCI Emerging Markets Index is made up of common stocks of companies located in emerging markets around the world.

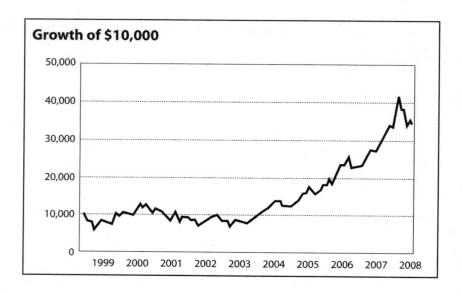

Holdings

Number of Holdings	947
Total Net Assets	$23.9 billion

Top Ten Holdings

- OAO Gazprom ADR
- China Mobile (Hong Kong) Ltd.
- Petroleo Brasileiro SA Pfd.
- Petroleo Brasileiro SA
- America Movil SA de CV
- Samsung Electronics Co., Ltd.
- Companhia Vale do Rio Doce Pfd. Class A
- Reliance Industries Ltd.
- Companhia Vale do Rio Doce
- Teva Pharmaceutical Industries Ltd.

Risk Attributes

TABLE A.18   Historic Volatility Measures as of 03/31/2008

Benchmark	R-squared*	Beta*
Spliced Emerging Markets Index	0.98	0.97
MSCI AC World Index ex USA	0.87	1.49

*R-squared and beta are calculated from trailing 36-month fund returns relative to the associated benchmark.

Management

Duane F. Kelly, Principal

- Portfolio manager
- Advised the fund since 1994
- Worked in investment management since 1989
- B.S., La Salle University

Investment Policy

The fund may invest in derivatives, including futures and options contracts. These contracts may be used to keep cash on hand to meet shareholder redemptions while simulating investment in a market index, to make trading easier, or to reduce costs by buying futures instead of actual stocks when futures are cheaper. Losses (or gains) involving futures and options contracts can be substantial—in part because a relatively small price movement in a contract may result in an immediate and substantial loss (or gain) for the fund. Similar risks exist for warrants, convertible securities, and swap agreements. For this reason, the fund will not use such investments for speculative purposes.

The fund may enter into forward currency contracts and foreign futures contracts to maintain the same currency exposure as its target index. However, the fund will not use these contracts for speculative purposes or as a hedge against currency fluctuations.

To earn additional income, the fund may lend its investment securities on a short- or long-term basis to qualified institutional investors.

Who Should Invest

- Investors seeking to further diversify a portfolio of U.S. securities
- Investors seeking long-term growth of capital
- Investors with a long-term investment horizon (at least five years)

Who Should Not Invest

- Investors unwilling to accept significant fluctuations in share price
- Investors seeking significant dividend income

Minimums

TABLE A.19 Minimums

	Initial Minimum	Additional Investments
General Account	$3,000	$100
IRA	$3,000	$100
UGMAs/UTMAs	$3,000	$100
Education Savings Account	$2,000	$100

Expenses

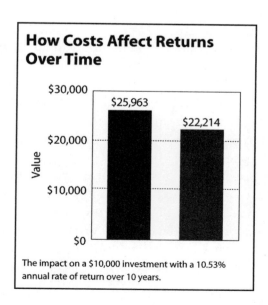

How Costs Affect Returns Over Time

$25,963

$22,214

The impact on a $10,000 investment with a 10.53% annual rate of return over 10 years.

TABLE A.20 Expenses

	Expense Ratio
Vanguard Emerging Markets Stock Index Inv	0.37%
Average Diversified Emerging Market Fund	2.01%

VANGUARD PRECIOUS METALS AND MINING FUND

Overview

Symbol	VGPMX
Expense Ratio	0.28%
Inception Date	5/23/1984
Yield	n/a
Admiral Shares	n/a

Description

The fund invests at least 80% of its assets in the stocks of foreign and U.S. companies principally engaged in the exploration, mining, development, fabrication, processing, marketing, or distribution of (or other activities related to) metals or minerals. The majority of these companies will be principally engaged in activities related to gold, silver, platinum, diamonds, or other precious and rare metals or minerals. The remaining companies will be principally engaged in activities related to nickel, copper, zinc, or other base and common metals or minerals. Precious and rare metals or minerals include those that are valued primarily for their use in nonindustrial or noncommercial applications. Base and common metals or minerals include those that are valued primarily for their use in ordinary industrial or commercial activities. Up to 100% of the fund's assets may be invested in foreign securities. The fund may also invest up to 20% of its assets directly in gold, silver, or other precious metal bullion and coins.

TABLE A.21 After-Tax Returns—Updated Quarterly as of 03/31/2008

	1 Year	3 Year	5 Year	10 Year	Since Inception 05/23/1984
Precious Metals and Mining					
Returns before Taxes	35.64%	39.79%	39.86%	23.10%	9.87%
Returns after Taxes on Distributions	32.51%	37.22%	37.60%	21.43%	—
Returns after Taxes on Distributions and Sale of Fund Shares	26.15%	34.18%	35.09%	20.23%	—
Average Precious Metals Fund					
Returns before Taxes	28.64%	32.43%	29.92%	16.78%	—
Returns after Taxes on Distributions	—	—	—	—	—
Returns after Taxes on Distributions and Sale of Fund Shares	—	—	—	—	—

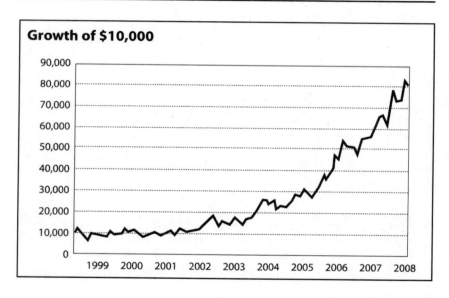

Holdings

Number of Holdings	39
Total Net Assets	$5.3 billion

Top Ten Holdings

- Eramet SLN
- Lonmin PLC
- Impala Platinum Holdings Ltd. ADR

- Barrick Gold Corp.
- Johnson Matthey PLC
- CONSOL Energy, Inc.
- Anglo Platinum Ltd. ADR
- Imerys SA
- Sims Group Ltd.
- Centerra Gold Inc.

Risk Attributes

TABLE A.22   Historic Volatility Measures as of 03/31/2008

Benchmark	R-squared*	Beta*
Spliced Precious Metals and Mining Index	0.88	0.79
Dow Jones Wilshire 5000 Composite Index	0.27	1.27

*R-squared and beta are calculated from trailing 36-month fund returns relative to the associated benchmark.

Management

Graham E. French

- Portfolio manager
- Advised the fund since 1991
- Worked in investment management since 1988
- B.S., University of Durham

Investment Policy

The fund may invest, to a limited extent, in derivatives. Generally speaking, a derivative is a financial contract whose value is based on the value of a traditional security, an asset, or a market index. The fund will not use derivatives for speculation or for the purpose of leveraging investment returns.

The fund may enter into foreign currency exchange contracts, which are types of futures contracts, to help protect its holdings against unfavorable changes in exchange rates. These contracts, however, will not prevent the fund's securities from falling in value during foreign market downswings. The fund will not enter into such contracts for speculative purposes. Under normal circumstances, the fund will not commit more than 20% of its assets to forward foreign currency exchange contracts.

Who Should Invest
- Investors seeking long-term growth of capital
- Investors with a long-term investment horizon (at least five years)

Who Should Not Invest
- Investors unwilling to accept significant fluctuations in share price
- Investors seeking a mutual fund that invests in a variety of industries

Minimums

TABLE A.23   Minimums

	Initial Minimum	Additional Investments
General Account	Closed	$100
IRA	Closed	$100
UGMAs/UTMAs	Closed	$100
Education Savings Account	Closed	$100

Expenses

How Costs Affect Returns Over Time

$30,000

$26,462

$23,067

$20,000

Value

$10,000

$0

The impact on a $10,000 investment with a 10.53% annual rate of return over 10 years.

TABLE A.24 Expenses

	Expense Ratio
Vanguard Precious Metals and Mining	0.28%
Average Precious Metals Fund	1.64%

VANGUARD REIT INDEX FUND

Overview

Symbol	VGSIX
Expense Ratio	0.20%
Inception Date	5/13/1996
Yield	4.4%
Admiral Shares	VGSLX

Description

The fund normally invests at least 98% of its assets in stocks issued
by equity real estate investment trusts (known as REITs) in an attempt
to parallel the investment performance of the MSCI U.S. REIT

TABLE A.25 After-Tax Returns—Updated Quarterly as of 03/31/2008

	1 Year	3 Year	5 Year	10 Year	Since Inception 05/13/1996
REIT Index Fund Inv					
Returns before Taxes	−17.48%	11.64%	17.76%	10.51%	12.79%
Returns after Taxes on Distributions	−18.46%	10.31%	16.10%	8.51%	10.76%
Returns after Taxes on Distributions and Sale of Fund Shares	−11.20%	9.41%	14.72%	7.93%	10.08%
Average Real Estate Fund					
Returns before Taxes	−18.36%	10.29%	17.49%	10.33%	—
Returns after Taxes on Distributions	—	—	—	—	—
Returns after Taxes on Distributions and Sale of Fund Shares	—	—	—	—	—

Index. The fund invests in the stocks that make up the index; the remaining assets are allocated to cash investments.

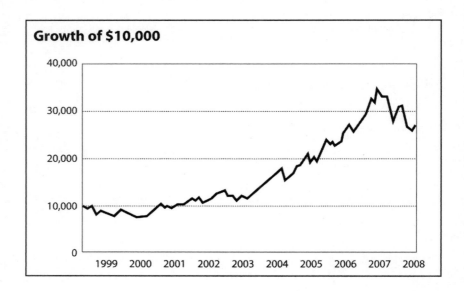

Holdings

Number of Holdings   97
Total Net Assets $8.9 billion

Top Ten Holdings

- Simon Property Group, Inc. REIT
- ProLogis REIT
- Vornado Realty Trust REIT
- Public Storage, Inc. REIT
- Equity Residential REIT
- Boston Properties, Inc. REIT
- Host Hotels & Resorts Inc. REIT
- General Growth Properties Inc. REIT
- Kimco Realty Corp. REIT
- Avalonbay Communities, Inc. REIT

Risk Attributes

TABLE A.26   Historic Volatility Measures

Benchmark	R-squared*	Beta*
Target REIT Composite	1.00	1.00
Dow Jones Wilshire 5000 Composite Index	0.35	1.07

*R-squared and beta are calculated from trailing 36-month fund returns relative to the associated benchmark.

Management

Gerard C. O'Reilly, Principal

- Portfolio manager
- Advised the fund since 1996
- Worked in investment management since 1992
- B.S., Villanova University

Investment Policy

The fund reserves the right to invest, to a limited extent, in stock futures and options contracts and in swap agreements. Stock futures and options contracts are traditional types of derivatives that are publicly traded on exchanges. Swap agreements are customized contracts that function like futures contracts but are not publicly traded on exchanges. These investments may be used to keep cash on hand to meet shareholder redemptions while simulating investment in stocks, to make trading easier, or to reduce costs by buying futures instead of actual stocks when futures are cheaper. The fund will not use futures, options, or swap agreements for speculative purposes.

Who Should Invest

- Investors seeking a high level of dividend income and long-term growth of capital
- Investors with a long-term investment horizon (at least five years)
- Investors seeking to add real estate exposure to their mix of stock, bond, and money market mutual funds

Who Should Not Invest

- Investors unwilling to accept significant fluctuations in share price
- Investors seeking a mutual fund that invests in a variety of industries

Minimums

TABLE A.27 Minimums

	Initial Minimum	Additional Investments
General Account	$3,000	$100
IRA	$3,000	$100
UGMAs/UTMAs	$3,000	$100
Education Savings Account	$2,000	$100

Expenses

How Costs Affect Returns Over Time

$26,675

$23,302

The impact on a $10,000 investment with a 10.53% annual rate of return over 10 years.

TABLE A.28 Expenses

	Expense Ratio
Vanguard REIT Index Fund Inv	0.20%
Average Real Estate Fund	1.54%

VANGUARD SHORT-TERM INVESTMENT-GRADE FUND

Overview

Symbol	VFSTX
Expense Ratio	0.21%
Inception Date	10/29/1982
Yield	4.31%
Admiral Shares	VFSUX

Description

The fund invests in a variety of high-quality and, to a lesser extent, medium-quality fixed income securities, at least 80% of which will be short- and intermediate-term investment-grade securities. High-quality fixed income securities are those rated the equivalent of A3 or better by Moody's Investors Service, Inc., or another independent rating agency; medium-quality fixed income securities are those rated the equivalent of Baa1, Baa2, or Baa3 by Moody's or

TABLE A.29 After-Tax Returns—Updated Quarterly as of 03/31/2008

	1 Year	3 Year	5 Year	10 Year	Since Inception 10/29/1982
Short-Term Invest-Grade Fund Inv					
Returns before Taxes	5.47%	4.88%	3.82%	5.02%	7.31%
Returns after Taxes on Distributions	3.70%	3.29%	2.36%	3.06%	—
Returns after Taxes on Distributions and Sale of Fund Shares	3.53%	3.23%	2.40%	3.07%	—
Average Short-Term Bond Fund					
Returns before Taxes	2.99%	3.39%	2.68%	4.29%	—
Returns after Taxes on Distributions	—	—	—	—	—
Returns after Taxes on Distributions and Sale of Fund Shares	—	—	—	—	—

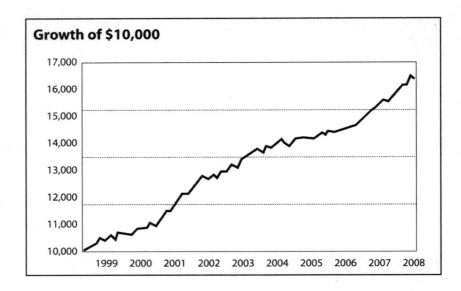

Growth of $10,000

another independent rating agency. (Investment-grade fixed income securities are those rated the equivalent of Baa3 and above by Moody's.) The fund is expected to maintain a dollar-weighted average maturity of one to three years.

Holdings

Number of Holdings	819
Total Net Assets	$20.3 billion

Bonds by Issuer

Asset–Backed	24.0%
Commercial Mortgage–Backed	0.0%
Finance	37.6%
Foreign	1.7%
Government Mortgage–Backed	3.6%
Industrial	25.3%
Other	1.5%
Short-Term Reserves	1.0%
Treasury/Agency	0.1%
Utilities	5.2%

Risk Attributes

TABLE A.30 Historic Volatility Measures as of 03/31/2008

Benchmark	R-squared*	Beta*
Lehman Brothers 1–5 Year U.S. Credit Index	0.95	0.75
Lehman U.S. Aggregate Bond Index	0.66	0.42

*R-squared and beta are calculated from trailing 36-month fund returns relative to the associated benchmark.

Management

Robert F. Auwaerter, Principal

- Portfolio manager
- Advised the fund since 1983
- Worked in investment management since 1978
- B.S., University of Pennsylvania
- M.B.A., Northwestern University

Investment Policy

The fund may invest no more than 30% of its assets in medium-quality bonds, preferred stocks, and convertible securities and no more than 5% of its assets in non–investment-grade and unrated bonds, preferred stocks, and convertible securities.

Futures, options, and other derivatives may represent up to 20% of the fund's total assets. The fund may invest up to 15% of its net assets in illiquid or restricted securities. For more information, please refer to the fund's prospectus.

Who Should Invest

- Investors seeking a high level of interest income and only slight fluctuations in the market value of their investment
- Investors seeking to balance a stock portfolio with a fixed income investment

Who Should Not Invest

- Investors seeking long-term growth of capital

Minimums

TABLE A.31   Minimums

	Initial Minimum	Additional Investments
General Account	$3,000	$100
IRA	$3,000	$100
UGMAs/UTMAs	$3,000	$100
Education Savings Account	$2,000	$100

Expenses

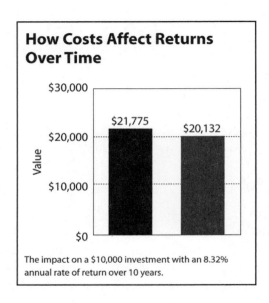

How Costs Affect Returns Over Time

$21,775 $20,132

The impact on a $10,000 investment with an 8.32% annual rate of return over 10 years.

TABLE A.32   Expenses

	Expense Ratio
Vanguard Short-Term Invest-Grade Fund Inv	0.21%
Average Short-Term Bond Fund	0.99%

VANGUARD HIGH-YIELD CORPORATE FUND

Overview

Symbol	VWEHX
Expense Ratio	0.25%

Inception Date 12/27/1978
Yield 8.25%
Admiral Shares VWEAX

Description

The fund invests mainly in a diversified group of high-yielding, higher-risk corporate bonds—commonly known as *junk bonds*—with medium- and lower-range credit-quality ratings. The fund invests at least 80% of its assets in corporate bonds that are rated below Baa by Moody's Investors Service, Inc., have an equivalent rating by any other independent bond-rating agency, or, if unrated, are determined to be of comparable quality by the fund's advisor. The fund may not invest more than 20% of its assets in any of the following, taken as a whole: bonds with credit ratings lower than B or the equivalent, convertible securities, and preferred stocks. High-yield bonds mostly have short- and intermediate-term maturities.

TABLE A.33 After-Tax Returns—Updated Quarterly as of 03/31/2008

	1 Year	3 Year	5 Year	10 Year	Since Inception 12/27/1978
High-Yield Corporate Fund Inv					
Returns before Taxes	−2.59%	4.07%	6.21%	4.39%	8.84%
Returns after Taxes on Distributions	−5.10%	1.49%	3.55%	1.35%	—
Returns after Taxes on Distributions and Sale of Fund Shares	−1.65%	2.00%	3.77%	1.84%	—
Average High-Yield Bond Fund					
Returns before Taxes	−4.65%	3.89%	7.47%	3.44%	—
Returns after Taxes on Distributions	—	—	—	—	—
Returns after Taxes on Distributions and Sale of Fund Shares	—	—	—	—	—

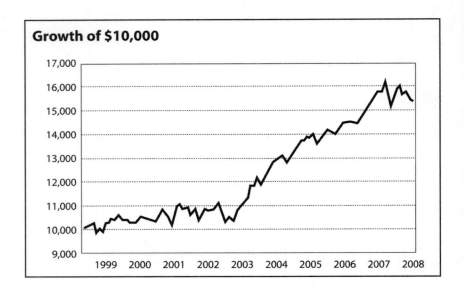

Growth of $10,000

Holdings

Number of Holdings	234
Total Net Assets	$8.7 billion

Includes Bonds from Issuers in:

Basic Industry	10.3%
Capital Goods	5.2%
Communication	19.5%
Consumer Cyclical	16.2%
Consumer Noncyclical	11.8%
Energy	10.1%
Finance	3.9%
Industrial Other	0.1%
Technology	1.7%
Transportation	2.9%
Treasury/Agency	4.9%
Utilities	13.4%

Risk Attributes

TABLE A.34 Historic Volatility Measures as of 03/31/2008

Benchmark	R-squared*	Beta*
Lehman U.S. Corporate High-Yield Bond Index	0.93	0.89
Lehman U.S. Aggregate Bond Index	0.02	0.23

*R-squared and beta are calculated from trailing 36-month fund returns relative to the associated benchmark.

Management

Earl E. McEvoy, Senior Vice President and Partner

- Portfolio manager
- Advised the fund since 1984
- Worked in investment management since 1972
- B.A., Dartmouth College
- M.B.A., Columbia Business School

Michael L. Hong, CFA, Vice President

- Portfolio manager
- Advised the fund since 2008
- Worked in investment management since 1997
- A.B., Harvard College

Investment Policy

The fund may invest in repurchase agreements. These are contracts in which a U.S. commercial bank or securities dealer sells government securities and agrees to repurchase them on a specific date and at a specific price.

The fund may invest in securities of foreign issuers, but all such securities must be denominated in U.S. dollars. The fund reserves the right to invest, to a limited extent, in stock futures and options contracts, which are traditional types of derivatives.

To earn additional income, the fund may lend its investment securities on a short- or long-term basis to qualified institutional investors.

Who Should Invest

- Investors seeking a high level of dividend income
- Investors seeking modest long-term growth of capital
- Investors with a long-term investment horizon (at least five years)

Who Should Not Invest

- Investors unwilling to accept significant fluctuations in share price
- Investors seeking an investment in high-quality bonds

Minimums

TABLE A.35   Minimums

	Initial Minimum	Additional Investments
General Account	$3,000	$100
IRA	$3,000	$100
UGMAs/UTMAs	$3,000	$100
Education Savings Account	$2,000	$100

Expenses

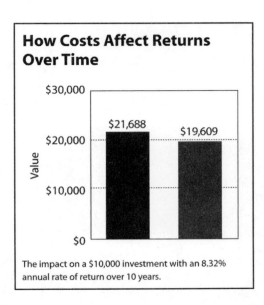

How Costs Affect Returns Over Time

$21,688

$19,609

The impact on a $10,000 investment with an 8.32% annual rate of return over 10 years.

TABLE A.36 Expenses

	Expense Ratio
Vanguard High-Yield Corporate Fund Inv	0.25%
Average High-Yield Bond Fund	1.25%

VANGUARD INFLATION-PROTECTED SECURITIES FUND

Overview

Symbol	VIPSX
Expense Ratio	0.20%
Inception Date	6/29/2000
Yield	0.82%
Admiral Shares	VAIPX

Description

The fund invests at least 80% of its assets in inflation-indexed bonds issued by the U.S. government, its agencies and instrumentalities, and corporations. The fund may invest in bonds of any maturity; however, its dollar-weighted average maturity is expected to be in a range of 7 to 20 years. At a minimum, all bonds purchased by the fund will be rated "investment-grade."

TABLE A.37 After-Tax Returns—Updated Quarterly as of 03/31/2008

	1 Year	3 Year	5 Year	10 Year	Since Inception 06/29/2000
Inflation-Protected Securities Fund Inv					
Returns before Taxes	14.78%	6.71%	6.65%	—	8.51%
Returns after Taxes on Distributions	12.44%	4.81%	4.85%	—	6.66%
Returns after Taxes on Distributions and Sale of Fund Shares	9.46%	4.57%	4.63%	—	6.24%
Average Inflation-Protected Bond Fund					
Returns before Taxes	12.65%	5.80%	5.79%	6.87%	—
Returns after Taxes on Distributions	—	—	—	—	—
Returns after Taxes on Distributions and Sale of Fund Shares	—	—	—	—	—

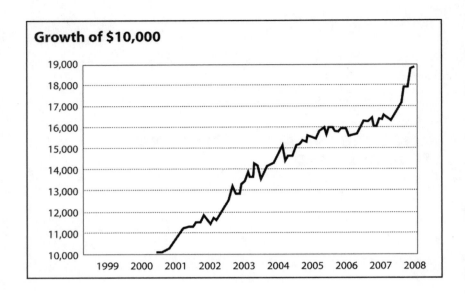

Growth of $10,000

Holdings

Number of Holdings	25
Total Net Assets	$14.7 billion

Risk Attributes

TABLE A.38   Historic Volatility Measures as of 03/31/2008

Benchmark	R-squared*	Beta*
Lehman U.S. Treasury Inflation Notes Index	1.00	0.97
Lehman U.S. Aggregate Bond Index	0.75	1.51

*R-squared and beta are calculated from trailing 36-month fund returns relative to the associated benchmark.

Management

John Hollyer, CFA, Principal

- Portfolio manager
- Advised the fund since 2000
- Worked in investment management since 1987
- B.S., University of Pennsylvania

Kenneth E. Volpert, CFA, Principal, Head of Taxable Bond Group

- Portfolio manager
- Advised the fund since 2000
- Worked in investment management since 1981
- B.S., University of Illinois
- M.B.A., University of Chicago

Investment Policy

Up to 20% of the fund's assets may be invested in holdings that are not inflation-indexed. The fund will make such investments primarily when inflation-indexed bonds are less attractive. The fund's non–inflation-indexed holdings may include the following:

- Corporate debt obligations
- U.S. government and agency bonds
- Cash investments
- Futures, options, and other derivatives
- Restricted or illiquid securities
- Mortgage dollar rolls

The fund may invest up to 20% of its total assets in bond futures contracts, options, credit swaps, interest rate swaps, and other types of derivatives. These contracts may be used to keep cash on hand to meet shareholder redemptions or other needs while simulating full investment in bonds, to reduce transaction costs, for hedging purposes, or to add value when these instruments are favorably priced. Losses (or gains) involving futures can be substantial—in part because a relatively small price movement in a futures contract may result in an immediate and substantial loss (or gain) for the fund. Similar risks exist for other types of derivatives. For this reason, the fund will not use derivatives for speculative purposes or as leveraged investments that magnify the gains or losses of an investment.

Restricted securities are privately placed securities that generally can only be sold to qualified institutional buyers and, hence, could be difficult for the fund to convert to cash, if needed. The fund will not invest more than 15% of its assets in such illiquid securities.

Mortgage dollar rolls are transactions in which a fund sells mortgage-backed securities to a dealer and simultaneously agrees to purchase similar securities in the future at a predetermined price. These transactions simulate an investment in mortgage-backed securities and have the potential to enhance a fund's returns and reduce its administrative burdens, compared with holding mortgage-backed securities directly. These transactions may increase a fund's portfolio turnover rate. Mortgage dollar rolls will be used only if consistent with a fund's investment objective and risk profile.

Who Should Invest

- Investors seeking a bond fund that provides inflation protection
- Investors seeking additional portfolio diversification that inflation-indexed securities can offer

Who Should Not Invest

- Investors unwilling to accept some volatility in income distributions
- Investors unwilling to tolerate modest fluctuations in share price
- Investors seeking long-term growth of capital

Minimums

TABLE A.39 Minimums

	Initial Minimum	Additional Investments
General Account	$3,000	$100
IRA	$3,000	$100
UGMAs/UTMAs	$3,000	$100
Education Savings Account	$2,000	$100

Expenses

How Costs Affect Returns Over Time

The impact on a $10,000 investment with an 8.32% annual rate of return over 10 years.

TABLE A.40   Expenses

	Expense Ratio
Vanguard Inflation-Protected Securities Fund Inv	0.20%
Average Inflation-Protected Bond Fund	1.02%

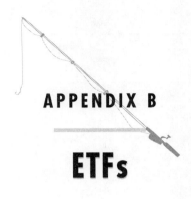

APPENDIX B

ETFs

Exchange-traded funds are a relatively new investment vehicle, as you can see from the inception dates for the funds below. You may notice that the stated performance of these funds varies greatly in some cases from similar mutual funds offered by the Vanguard Group. Please understand that these discrepancies are due primarily to their short life span and not to any dramatic difference in their composition or management. Going forward, the annual returns generated by these exchange-traded funds and the Vanguard mutual funds should be similar.

VANGUARD TOTAL STOCK MARKET ETF

Overview

Symbol	VTI
Expense Ratio	0.07%
Inception Date	5/24/2001

Description

Vanguard Total Stock Market ETF is an exchange-traded share class of the Vanguard Total Stock Market Index Fund. It employs a passive management—or indexing—investment approach designed to track

TABLE B.1 Performance Returns before Taxes

1 Year	3 Year	5 Year	Since Inception
−5.69%	6.31%	12.39	3.15%

the performance of the MSCI U.S. Broad Market Index, which represents 99.5% or more of the total market capitalization of all of the U.S. common stocks regularly traded on the New York and American Stock Exchanges and the Nasdaq over-the-counter market. The fund typically holds the largest 1,200 to 1,300 stocks in its target index (covering nearly 95% of the index's total market capitalization) and a representative sample of the remaining stocks. The fund holds a range of securities that, in the aggregate, approximates the full index in terms of key characteristics. These key characteristics include industry weightings and market capitalization, as well as certain financial measures, such as price/earnings ratio and dividend yield.

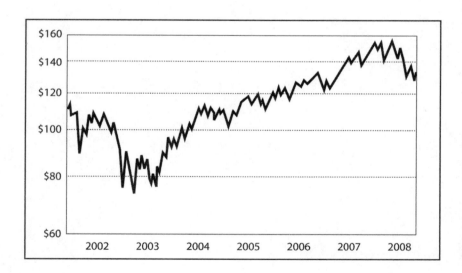

Holdings

Number of Holdings	3,552
Median Market Cap	$1.5 billion
Fund Total Net Assets	$13.5 billion

Top Ten Holdings

- ExxonMobil Corp.
- General Electric Co.
- Microsoft Corp.
- AT&T Inc.
- Procter & Gamble Co.
- Chevron Corp.
- Johnson & Johnson
- Bank of America Corp.
- IBM
- Altria Group, Inc.

VANGUARD SMALL-CAP ETF

Overview

Symbol	VB
Expense Ratio	0.10%
Inception Date	1/26/2004

Description

Vanguard Small-Cap ETF is an exchange-traded share class of the Vanguard Small-Cap Index Fund. It employs a passive management—or indexing—investment approach designed to track the performance of the MSCI U.S. Small-Cap 1750 Index, a broadly diversified index of stocks of smaller U.S. companies. The fund attempts to replicate the target index by investing all, or substantially all, of its assets in the stocks that make up the index, holding each stock in approximately the same proportion as its weighting in the index.

TABLE B.2 Performance Returns before Taxes

1 Year	3 Year	5 Year	Since Inception
−11.10%	6.11%	—	6.13%

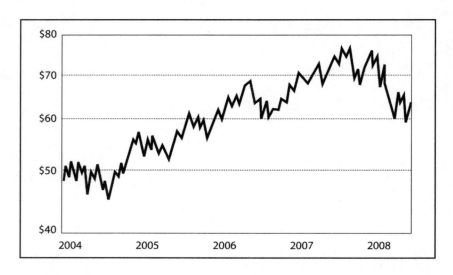

Holdings

Number of Holdings	1727
Median Market Cap	$1.5 billion
Fund Total Net Assets	$13.5 billion

Top Ten Holdings

- Cleveland–Cliffs Inc
- Cabot Oil & Gas Corp.
- Helmerich & Payne, Inc.
- Priceline.com, Inc.
- FMC Corp.
- Terra Industries, Inc.
- Illumina, Inc.
- Forest Oil Corp.
- Reliance Steel & Aluminum Co.
- Bucyrus International, Inc.

VANGUARD EUROPEAN ETF

Overview

Symbol	VGK
Expense Ratio	0.12%
Inception Date	3/4/2005

Description

Vanguard European ETF is an exchange-traded share class of the Vanguard European Stock Index Fund. It employs a passive management—or indexing—investment approach by investing all, or substantially all, of its assets in the common stocks included in the MSCI Europe Index. The index is made up of common stocks of companies located in 16 European countries. The countries with the largest capitalization weightings in the index are the United Kingdom, France, Switzerland, and Germany; others represented are Austria, Belgium, Denmark, Finland, Greece, Ireland, Italy, the Netherlands, Norway, Portugal, Spain, and Sweden.

TABLE B.3 Performance Returns before Taxes

1 Year	3 Year	5 Year	Since Inception
3.00%	14.93%	—	13.25%

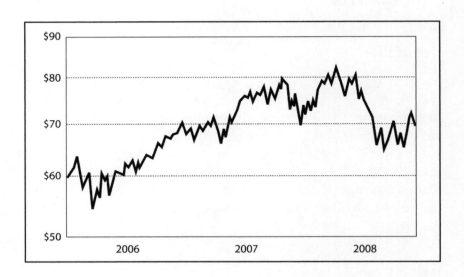

Holdings

Number of Holdings	634
Fund Total Net Assets	$33.4 billion

Top Ten Holdings

- BP PLC
- Nestle SA
- HSBC Holdings PLC
- Vodafone Group PLC
- Total SA
- Nokia Oyj
- Roche Holdings AG
- Telefonica SA
- GlaxoSmithKline PLC
- E.On AG

VANGUARD PACIFIC ETF

Overview

Symbol	VPL
Expense Ratio	0.12%
Inception Date	3/4/2005

Description

Vanguard Pacific ETF is an exchange-traded share class of the Vanguard Pacific Stock Index Fund. It employs a passive management—or indexing—investment approach by investing all, or substantially all, of its assets in the common stocks included in the MSCI Pacific Index. The index consists of common stocks of companies located in Japan, Australia, Hong Kong, Singapore, and New Zealand. The countries with the largest capitalization weightings in the index are Japan and Australia.

TABLE B.4 Performance Returns before Taxes

1 Year	3 Year	5 Year	Since Inception
8.27%	10.32%	—	8.75%

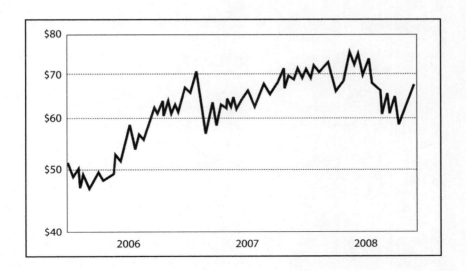

Holdings

Number of Holdings	590
Fund Total Net Assets	$15.3 billion

Top Ten Holdings

- Toyota Motor Corp.
- BHP Billiton Ltd.
- Mitsubishi UFJ Financial Group
- Commonwealth Bank of Australia
- Nintendo Co.
- Canon, Inc.
- Honda Motor Co., Ltd.
- Sumitomo Mitsui Financial Group, Inc.
- Sony Corp.
- Takeda Pharmaceutical Co. Ltd.

VANGUARD EMERGING MARKETS ETF

Overview

Symbol	VWO
Expense Ratio	0.25%
Inception Date	3/4/2005

Description

Vanguard Emerging Markets ETF is an exchange-traded share class of the Vanguard Emerging Markets Stock Index Fund. It employs a passive management—or indexing—investment approach by investing substantially all (normally about 95%), of its assets in the common stocks included in the MSCI Emerging Markets Index. The MSCI Emerging Markets Index is made up of common stocks of companies located in emerging markets around the world.

TABLE B.5 Performance Returns before Taxes

1 Year	3 Year	5 Year	Scince Inception
21.82%	28.15%	—	24.60%

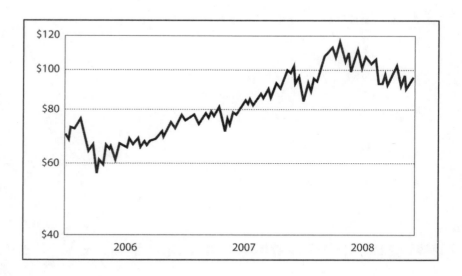

Holdings

Number of Holdings	947
Fund Total Net Assets	$23.9 billion

Top Ten Holdings

- OAO Gazprom ADR
- China Mobile Ltd.
- Petroleo Brasileiro SA Pfd.
- Petroleo Brasileiro SA
- America Movil SA de CV
- Samsung Electronics Co., Ltd.
- Companhia Vale do Rio Doce Pfd. Class A
- Reliance Industries Ltd.
- Companhia Vale do Rio Doce
- Teva Pharmaceutical Industries Ltd.

MARKET VECTORS GOLD MINERS ETF

Overview

Symbol	GDX
Expense Ratio	0.68%
Inception Date	5/16/2006

Description

The Gold Miners ETF seeks to track the performance of gold- and silver-mining companies as represented in the Amex Gold Miners Index. The Amex Gold Miners Index includes common stocks or ADRs of selected companies involved in mining for gold or silver ore. The index consists of 34 equities, representing a diversified blend of small-, mid-, and large-capitalization mining companies. As such, the fund is subject to the risks of investing in this sector.

TABLE B.6 Performance Returns before Taxes

1 Year	3 Year	5 Year	Since Inception
35.00%	—	—	18.67%

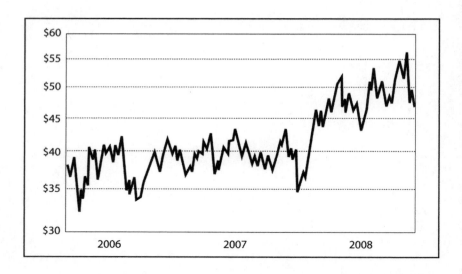

Holdings

Number of Holdings	37
Average Market Cap	$5.7 billion*
Fund Total Net Assets	$2.19 billion

Top Ten Holdings

- Barrick Gold Corp.
- Goldcorp, Inc
- Newmont Mining Corp.
- Kinross Gold Corp.
- Yamana Gold, Inc.
- Compania de Minas Buenaventura SA
- Agnico-Eagle Mines LTD.
- Harmony Gold Mining Co.
- Gold Fields LTD.
- Silver Wheaton Corp.

*Represents the average index.

VANGUARD REIT ETF

Overview

Symbol	VNQ
Expense Ratio	0.10%
Inception Date	9/23/2004

Description

Vanguard REIT ETF is an exchange-traded share class of the Vanguard REIT Index Fund. It employs a passive management—or indexing—investment approach designed to track the performance of the MSCI U.S. REIT Index, a benchmark of U.S. property trusts that covers about two-thirds of the value of the entire U.S. REIT market. The fund intends to remain at least 98% invested in REIT stocks; the remaining assets will be in cash investments to maintain liquidity for shareholder redemptions. In seeking to match the index, the advisor does not try to predict or profit from

TABLE B.7 Performance Returns before Taxes

1 Year	3 Year	5 Year	Since Inception
17.39%	11.78%	—	12.49%

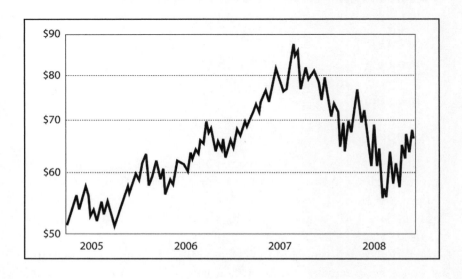

changes in the direction of the REIT market. The fund's cash holding will result in small differences between the returns of the fund and those of the MSCI U.S. REIT Index.

Holdings

Number of Holdings	97
Average Market Cap	$5.0 billion
Fund Total Net Assets	$8.9 billion

Top Ten Holdings

- Simon Property Group, Inc. REIT
- ProLogis REIT
- Vornado Realty Trust REIT
- Public Storage, Inc. REIT
- Equity Residential REIT
- Boston Properties, Inc. REIT
- Host Hotels & Resorts Inc. REIT
- General Growth Properties Inc. REIT
- Kimco Realty Corp. REIT
- Avalonbay Communities, Inc. REIT

VANGUARD TOTAL BOND MARKET ETF

Overview

Symbol	BND
Expense Ratio	0.11%
Inception Date	4/3/2007

Description

The fund employs a passive management—or indexing—investment approach designed to track the performance of the Lehman U.S. Aggregate Bond Index. This index measures a wide spectrum of public, investment-grade, taxable, fixed income securities in the United States—including government, corporate, and international dollar-denominated bonds, as well as mortgage-backed and asset-backed securities, all with maturities of more than one year.

The fund invests by sampling the index, meaning that it holds a range of securities that, in the aggregate, approximate the full index in terms of key risk factors and other characteristics. All of the fund's investments will be selected through the sampling process, and at least 80% of the fund's assets will be invested in bonds held in the index. The fund maintains a dollar-weighted average maturity consistent with that of the index, which currently ranges between 5 and 10 years.

TABLE B.8 Performance Returns before Taxes

1 Year	3 Year	5 Year	Since Inception
—	—	—	8.06%

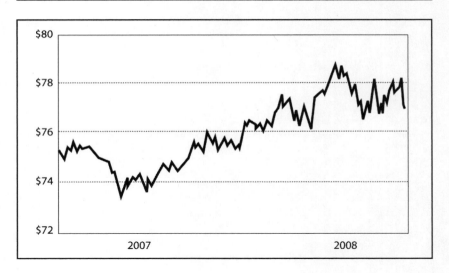

Holdings

Number of Holdings	37
Fund Total Net Assets	$54.9 billion

Holdings Following Types of Bonds

- Asset-backed
- Commercial mortgage–backed
- Finance
- Foreign
- Government mortgage–backed
- Industrial

- Treasury/agency
- Utilities
- Other

iSHARES iBOXX $ HIGH-YIELD CORPORATE BOND FUND

Overview

Symbol	HYG
Expense Ratio	0.50%
Inception Date	4/4/2007

Description

The iShares iBoxx $ High-Yield Corporate Bond Fund seeks investment results that correspond generally to the price and yield performance, before fees and expenses, of the iBoxx $ Liquid

TABLE B.9 Performance Returns before Taxes

1 Year	3 Year	5 Year	Since Inception
—	—	—	−1.89%

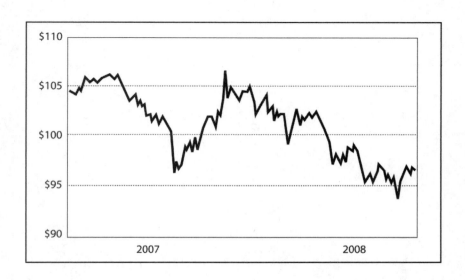

High-Yield Index, a corporate bond market index compiled by the International Index Company Limited.

Holdings

Number of Holdings	50
Fund Total Net Assets	$525 billion

Top Ten Holdings

- Freeport–McMoran C & G
- Sungard Data Systems Inc.
- Crown Americas LLC
- HCA Inc
- Peabody Energy Corporation
- Community Health Systems Inc
- El Paso Corp.
- Terex Corporation
- Edison Mission Energy
- Mirant North America LLC

iSHARES LEHMAN TIPS BOND FUND

Overview

Symbol	TIP
Expense Ratio	0.20%
Inception Date	12/4/2003

Description

The iShares Lehman U.S. Treasury Inflation-Protected Securities Bond Fund seeks results that correspond generally to the price and yield performance, before fees and expenses, of the inflation-protected sector of the U.S. Treasury market as defined by the Lehman Brothers U.S. Treasury TIPS Index.

TABLE B.10 Performance Returns before Taxes

1 Year	3 Year	5 Year	Since Inception
14.78%	6.63%	—	6.71%

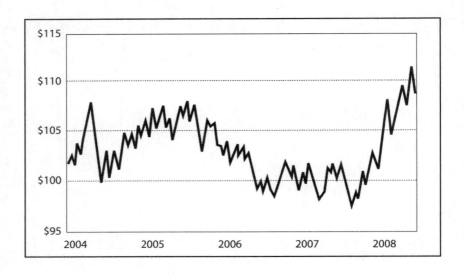

Holdings

Number of Holdings	24
Fund Total Net Assets	$6.6 billion

ABOUT THE AUTHOR

Alexander Green is the investment director of The Oxford Club. A Wall Street veteran, he has over two decades' experience as a financial writer, research analyst, investment advisor, and professional portfolio manager.

Under his direction, The Oxford Club's portfolios have beaten the Wilshire 5000 Index by a margin of more than three to one. The *Oxford Club Communique,* whose portfolio he directs, is ranked third in the nation for risk-adjusted returns over the past five years by the independent *Hulbert Financial Digest.*

Mr. Green has written for several leading financial publications and has appeared on many radio and television shows, including Fox News, CNBC, and *The O'Reilly Factor.* He has also been profiled by *Forbes, Kiplinger's Personal Finance,* Marketwatch.com, and other major media.

He is chairman of Investment U, an Internet-based research service with more than 300,000 readers. Investment U offers cutting-edge financial commentary and is dedicated to increasing financial literacy, revealing "What No Books, No Schools, No Brokers Will Teach You."

He currently writes and directs the *Oxford Insight* e-letter and three elite trading services: the Momentum Alert, the Insider Alert, and the ADR Alert.

Mr. Green is also the editor of the free, twice-weekly e-letter *Spiritual Wealth,* offering ideas about how to live a richer, more meaningful life. As Henry Ward Beecher famously said, "No man can tell whether he is rich or poor by turning to his ledger . . . He is rich according to what he is, not according to what he has."

Mr. Green is also a top-rated speaker at financial conferences around the world.

Web sites

- www.OxfordClub.com
- www.InvestmentU.com
- www.SpiritualWealth.com

E-mail address: editor@spiritualwealth.com

INDEX

INDEX **237**

Special Offer for

The Gone Fishin' Portfolio Readers

Get a **47% discount** on a membership to Alexander Green's investment letter, *The Oxford Club Communiqué*.

As a member, you will receive 22 issues of the *Communiqué* plus the 24-page Annual Investors' Forecast edition for only $79.

In the letter, Alex makes and reviews recommendations for the Oxford Trading Portfolio, which has garnered national attention for its impressive track record.

The Hulbert Financial Digest tracks the returns of the Oxford Trading Portfolio – and the returns of 180 other investment letters – and found that the Oxford Trading Portfolio's five-year risk-adjusted returns put it among the top five investment newsletters in the country.

You will also receive the twice-weekly *Oxford Insight* e-letter, which includes timely investment updates on recommendations, including updates on the funds that comprise the Gone Fishin' Portfolio.

We normally offer this annual subscription for $149 – but we're extending a special lower rate to readers of *The Gone Fishin' Portfolio*.

To place your order immediately, just call
877-806-4508 or 915-849-4617
and give this Priority Book Code: IOXFJ801